Windsurfing
With Ken Winner

A Complete Illustrated Guide to a Fast-Growing Sport

Windsurfing
With Ken Winner

KEN WINNER & ROGER JONES
PREFACE BY JAMES R. DRAKE

HARPER & ROW, PUBLISHERS
SAN FRANCISCO

Cambridge   London
Hagerstown   Mexico City
Philadelphia São Paulo
New York   Sydney
1817

Library of Congress Cataloging in Publication Data

Winner, Ken.
  Windsurfing with Ken Winner.

  Includes index.
  1. Windsurfing.   I. Jones, Roger, joint author.
II. Title.

GV811.63.W56W56   1980   797.1'7   80-8399

ISBN 0-06-250971-3

Printed and bound in Canada by
The Hunter Rose Company Ltd.

80 81 82 83 84 10 9 8 7 6 5 4 3 2 1

CONTENTS

ACKNOWLEDGEMENTS

Thanks go to the many people who helped bring this project to its successful completion.

In particular, thanks to the following (in alphabetical order):

- Alan Adelkind
- Lionel Broderick
- Dennis Davidson
- James R. Drake
- June Everett
- Alison Fitts
- Doug Hunt
- Cort Larned
- Colin Perry
- Mark Robinson
- Rhonda Smith
- Suzi Smyth
- Larry Stanley
- Glenn Taylor
- William Whidden
- Michael Worek

Racing consultant:
Alan Adelkind, Coach, Canadian Olympic 470 Sailing Team

To L.

James R. Drake, aeronautical engineer, is responsible for much of the problem solving associated with developing the free-sail system

PREFACE

Roger called me one afternoon and asked if he could come by to discuss this project of his and Ken's, a new book on windsurfing. He wanted to check certain details about the early days. I'd met Ken before at a number of regattas, but Roger was a new face. This new face soon proved to be owned by an energetic and inspired young man dedicated to the project of bringing into print a comprehensive technical and experiential picture of the sport of windsurfing.

When later we met and the full scope of the book became apparent, I again realized how far the sport had come in the twelve years since that day in 1967 when I taught myself to windsurf. Roger went further and reminded me of the prophetic words I wrote in 1969 to the effect that "It could be that there are still many useful maneuvers and techniques of greater difficulty which are as yet undiscovered," an understatement of the first magnitude as proved on the pages following. When I wrote that sentence, I really had no idea what youth and talent could do in expanding the dimensions of the sport. In fact, the sport itself, while acknowledging contributions by early pioneers, owes far more to its current legion of enthusiasts.

Some of these enthusiasts, like Ken with his extraordinary skill, are able to innovate and execute truly astonishing moves. Others learn and popularize those moves until they seem as natural as the tack, the jibe . . . and the inevitable unscheduled drop-out. In this same spirit, the spirit of exploring and then sharing, I think the reader will find this book to be an exceptionally good attempt at communication not only between expert and student, but also between experts anxious to keep pace with the sport's explosive expansion. I'm delighted that Roger and Ken have made such an attempt.

James R. Drake

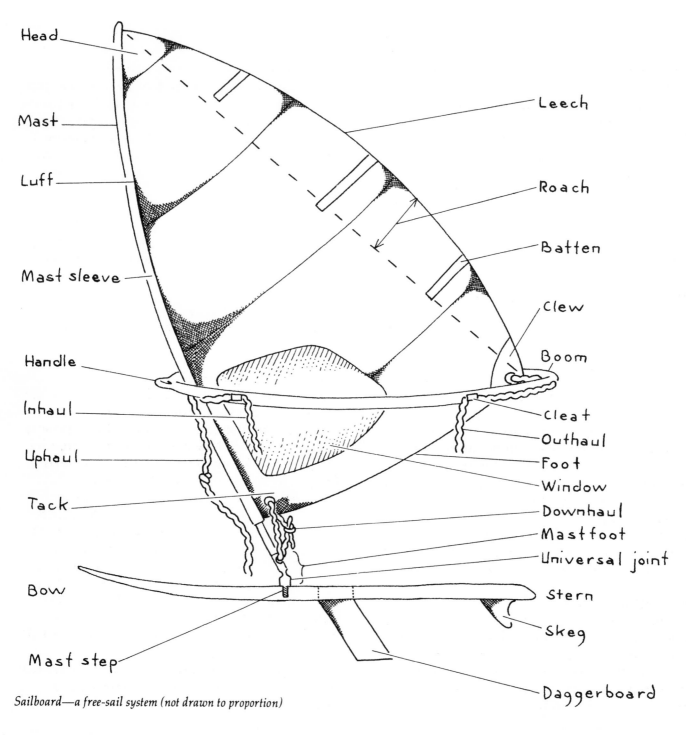

Head

Mast

Luff

Mast sleeve

Handle

Inhaul

Uphaul

Tack

Bow

Mast step

Leech

Roach

Batten

Clew

Boom

Cleat

Outhaul

Foot

Window

Downhaul

Mastfoot

Universal joint

Stern

Skeg

Daggerboard

Sailboard—a free-sail system (not drawn to proportion)

INTRODUCTION

THE WIND IS FREE

With skill your sailboard becomes an extension of your body, and sailing it brings you closer to the elements of wind and water than perhaps anything else can. The magic usually starts that first time you keep your balance for a few hundred meters. The surge of adrenaline gives a high worth all the dunkings. So you keep practicing. Whenever the wind is up you want to be out on the water. You put in the hours and get to handle higher wind and waves. Then it comes, the moment you are hiked far out in a 20-knot breeze, the sail pulled way over you like a wing and the board planing back to the daggerboard, and suddenly it all feels EFFORTLESS. You don't know whether you are flying, sailing or surfing. You just know it feels so good you want to keep doing it forever.

Apart from such highs, some of the reasons for the sport's growing popularity are its relative cheapness, convenience and its appeal to all ages and kinds of people. The sport is fairly inexpensive because most of the cost is in the initial purchase. There aren't the expensive follow-up costs associated with sports like skiing. Since sailboards are light and compact they can usually be stored at home, conveniently carried on car roofs, and launched single-handed.

In addition, many have found windsurfing an excellent way of meeting people—people of all ages and types. Youngest we know of started windsurfing at age five; oldest is a man in his seventies. And it is a misconception that strength is necessary. To rival the champions you'll certainly need to be fit. But from the statistics that over half those passing certified windsurfing courses are women, you can tell that technique is the key, not brute strength.

A word on what to expect when starting: expect to fall a fair number of times. What the heck, you only get wet. Wear a good wet suit and you'll keep warm even in chilly conditions. If you start on flat water in light wind, following the correct procedure, it usually takes around two hours to learn the rudiments of balance and sailing back and forth on a reach.

In many areas you'll find a friendly windsurfing community. Sail with them. You'll learn faster by observing experienced sailors closely and asking for advice now and again. Have an experienced sailor watch you sail occasionally to correct and avoid bad habits.

To become expert add one essential element. Practice. Hundreds of hours. You can afford it— the wind is free.

FATHERS OF THE SPORT

In the U.S. in the mid-1960s, there appeared two published accounts of "sailboards" carrying hand-held sails. The first account was by a Pennsylvania inventor named S. Newman Darby, the other by (wouldn't you know it) a southern Californian, Jim Drake, describing efforts by himself and others, notably Hoyle Schweitzer, the current U.S. manufacturer and licensor of the Windsurfer.

Many people now claim to have developed sailboards prior to this. Almost every year at the Miami boat show, for example, an old character would show up at the Windsurfer booth to claim he invented the sport several decades before the patented Windsurfer appeared. If these prior inventions indeed existed, they were not patented, nor were they widely known.

S. Newman Darby's rather clumsy, unpatented design was published in *Popular Science*, August 1965, in an article headed "Sailboarding: Exciting

Hoyle and Diane Schweitzer

New Water Sport for High-speed Water Fun . . .
A Sport So New That Fewer Than 10 People
Have Yet Mastered It." A square-rigger, Darby's
sailboard was designed to be pushed by the wind.
You steered "by pivoting the mast in its socket,
tilting (the) sail." A limited number were sold
around 1965 but the design didn't catch on. It was
from the southern Californians that the patented
Windsurfer came, the elegant product on which
today's competing free-sail systems are modeled.

With a simplicity that itself is beautiful, the
Windsurfer consists merely of a long slim hull
with tail fin (skeg), daggerboard and an unsup-
ported, universally hinged sail with wishbone
booms. No mechanical devices, no pulleys or
levers come between you and the elements. No
shrouds support the rig, no rudder steers you.
That's why windsurfing differs from traditional
sailing so markedly, and brings you into such
exciting, direct contact with the elements: the

skipper supports the sail by holding the booms,
steers by utilizing the universal joint to vary the
sail position. Hence the technical term "free-sail"
system.

Much of the problem solving associated with
developing the free-sail system was done by Jim
Drake, an aeronautical engineer. Drake reports
that the concept grew out of conversations with a
scientist friend, Fred Payne, beginning in 1961[*].
Another contributor to the development of this
free-sail system, besides Hoyle Schweitzer, was
Allen Parducci.

The idea of an articulated mast, which actually
led to the patent, was conceived by Jim while
driving westbound, alone, on the San Bernadino

---

[*]James R. Drake, *Wind Surfing—A New Concept in Sailing*, paper
presented at the first American Institute for Aeronautics
and Astronautics (AIAA) Technical Symposium on Sailboat
Design, Los Angeles, California, April 26, 1969, published
by RAND Corporation, Santa Monica, California.

Freeway. By early 1967 he was experimenting with two versions of a free-sail system, one with a fully articulated universal on the mast foot, the other with a mast attached rigidly to the dagger-board. The latter setup allowed the mast to be tilted fore and aft, the unit pivoting around the daggerboard so that the daggerboard rotated back as the mast rotated forward. (Both versions allowed the sail to swing around in a full circle.) Drake decided to go with the fully articulated universal. He and Schweitzer continued to experiment, and in 1969 Drake reported* that six different designs for the Baja-Board had been built and tested. These were given lighthearted names—for example, Big Red, The Door, and Yellow Submarine, "named because of its habit of sounding like an harpooned whale whenever the wind blew very strong."

Patent processes were initiated in a number of countries in 1968, and Schweitzer, who finalized the design of the Windsurfer, decided to go into business making the new craft. By 1970 he was producing a limited number of Baja-Boards, made of plastic foam coated with fiberglass.

A tenacious determined man, Schweitzer—aided throughout by his wife Diane—was able to keep the sport slowly progressing out of obscurity. But because of limited promotion and marketing, few people knew of windsurfing till 1973 when a Dutch textile manufacturer, Nijverdal Ten Cate, took a license to produce Windsurfers in Europe. There the sport caught on like wildfire, particularly in Germany. Dozens of companies stepped in to manufacture (most pirating the patent) and in the five years from 1973 to 1978 an estimated 150,000 sailboards (all brands) were sold in Europe—about twenty times as many as were sold in North America in the first decade of the sport.

Rapid growth in North America began in 1977 and 1978. Since then windsurfing's popularity has increased dramatically, and as more companies enter the market with competing sailboards the growth is becoming even more rapid.

GETTING STARTED

1

This chapter will enable you to teach yourself basic balance and maneuvering in three to six hours spread over three or four sessions. Some people will prefer to take instruction at a windsurfing school, but even these people will find useful backup to their learning here.

Windsurfing is not difficult to learn, provided you choose suitable conditions. Even your first wobbly attempt can be fun if you are properly prepared, so before you go out on the water, some pointers:

Initially, choose calm water and light steady winds (3 to 8 knots)

Ideally, learn on a shallow (3 to 4 feet deep) pond 100 to 200 yards across. This will be calm and you won't have far to walk back if (when) you fall prey to the good old "blown-downwind syndrome," as most of us have one time or another. Pick a place with a steady wind that is not disturbed by hills, tall buildings, trees, etc. A freaky wind whirling around obstacles can make learning tricky.

It is dangerous to learn on a large expanse of water in offshore winds

An offshore wind blows from land to water. When learning you inevitably drift with the wind and can end up far from land, unable to sail back. Avoid strong currents, too. A current in any direction adds to learning difficulty.

Stay close to land while learning

Select landmarks on shore as reference points. Check them frequently because you'll often lose track of time and circumstances when concentrating on sailing. Before you drift over 100 yards

from shore, kneel and paddle in. At first it's a good idea to tether the board to something on shore using 20 to 30 yards of light line tied through the daggerboard well, or around the daggerboard under the sailboard. Then you can pull yourself ashore.

Wear a wet suit

Even in warm water wear a wet suit (chapt. 5) as a precaution against hypothermia. Hypothermia or "exposure" is a lowered deep body temperature, which causes the body's vital functions to cease. It happens more easily than many people realize. Prolonged immersion in water as warm as 20°C. (68°F.) can cause loss of consciousness. Wet suits are fairly comfortable, and well worth the cost. It is surprising how warm you are kept by the thin layer of water trapped between the insulating neoprene and your body.

Wear deck shoes

Wear deck shoes if the deck is slippery and to avoid cut feet on shells, broken bottles, etc., under water. High-top shoes keep sand out best.

Always stay with the board

The board gives valuable flotation. If you can't sail back, paddle the board back. You can paddle faster than you can swim. And you'll be seen more readily on the board. Keep the sail rig and board together and if they're separated swim for the board first because it'll quickly drift away, whereas the mast and sail will remain relatively stationary. If you want to slow your drift downwind remember that the sail lying in the water acts as a sea anchor, and the deeper it lies the more it will slow your drift with the wind.

Fig. 1 *In light wind and flat water you can paddle the board with the boom resting on the back of the board*

Learn how to paddle the board

In flat water and light wind rest the boom on the back of the board to keep mast, boom ends and sail from dragging in the water, and kneel or lie on the board paddling with your hands. If you can't make progress against wind and waves, derig your board, rolling the sail and lashing it to the mast with the outhaul line and uphaul. Lay the mast lengthwise along the center of the board and lie on it facing forward. Paddle with both hands, breaststroke or crawl fashion, or sit on the board paddling with the daggerboard. This is harder than you'd expect, especially against strong wind or currents, so it's a good idea to practice once or twice. The mast without sail and booms on it makes an efficient paddle, but take care not to drop it. Unless it has plastic foam inside or the ends made watertight, your mast will sink—rapidly.

A life jacket is a sensible precaution if you feel unsure of yourself

In some areas life jackets are mandatory. Choose one that isn't bulky, preferably with a soft inner lining for comfort.

Identify wind direction before leaving shore

You should start sailing with your back to the wind, so clearly distinguish its direction by, for example, observing a flag or tossing something light like grass into the air.

LAUNCHING

In general, avoid scratching the equipment on rough surfaces by carrying the board and rigged sail to the water's edge. Don't place the board on the water first; it will quickly drift away. First take the sail to the water, carrying it over your head, boom lying along the direction of the wind, mast toward the wind. Place or throw the rig onto the water making sure it falls flat (fig. 2A).

Carry the board with the top toward your body, one hand in the mast step slot, the other hand on the other side of the board in the dagger-board slot or with the daggerboard in and holding the daggerboard (fig. 2B).

Fig. 2A *Carry sail over your head, booms aligned along wind direction*

WIND

Fig. 2B
Carry board with deck toward body, one hand in mast step slot, other hand over the board and in the bottom of the daggerboard well

Fig. 3 *Roger Jones demonstrates a popular form of beach launch*

An alternative, convenient way to launch from surfaces that won't scratch is to drag the rigged board by standing between the mast and board, the nose of the board under one arm, the uphaul in the other hand (fig. 3).

Whichever way you launch make sure that before you insert the daggerboard there's enough water to prevent it running aground. Particularly in earlier-model Windsurfers, without reinforcement in the daggerboard well, running aground can easily split the well. Then water gets into the board and can make the polyethylene skin delaminate from the foam.

LIFTING THE SAIL FROM THE WATER

With the daggerboard in and the mast base firmly in its slot (use tape on the mast base if necessary— see chapt. 2), arrange the board in the water so it is at right angles to the wind and points in the direction you intend to go, the sail lying in the water on the side farthest from the wind (leeward side). The sail should make a right angle with the board.

Now climb onto the board with your back to the wind, keeping your weight on the centerline.

Stand with the arches of your feet over the centerline, one foot either side of the universal joint. You'll find out just how easily the board tips as soon as you step off that centerline. Hold the end of the uphaul rope in one hand, leaving the

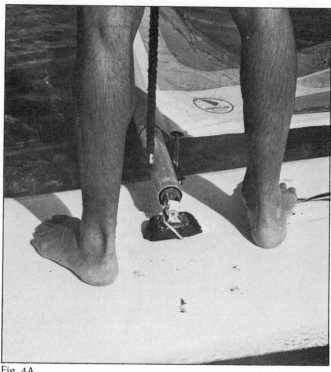

Fig. 4A
To lift the sail from the water, first stand with the arches of your feet over the centerline, one foot either side of the universal joint

Fig. 4B *Hold the uphaul rope in one hand, other hand free to help balance*

Fig. 5A *Lean your body backward and straighten your knees to lift the sail just enough for the water to run off*

Fig. 5B *Rapidly pull the sail toward you until the far end of the boom is completely out of the water*

other arm free to aid balance. Don't pull the sail up immediately: first get the feel of the board by rocking it from side to side with your ankles. You'll balance better if you keep your hips, knees and ankles loose. People tend to tense their legs on feeling the instability of the board, so work at relaxing.

If the sail is in the water on the side the wind is coming from (windward side), move it to the other side as follows: lift it slightly by putting your weight on the uphaul rope, and with the end of the boom just touching the water draw the mast across the back of the board (the booms tend to jam on the bow). Step around yourself with small steps till the mast is at a right angle to the board, on the leeward side.

Never try to lift the sail with your back bent. Squat down, pulling the uphaul taut. Then, by leaning your body backward and straightening your knees, lift the sail just enough for the water to run off. This way the thighs take the toughest strain, and as water runs off the sail and out of the sleeve, the rig lightens. Figure 5 illustrates this lifting process.

Fig. 5C *Hold the uphaul near the boom. Allow the sail to align itself downwind at right angles to the board*

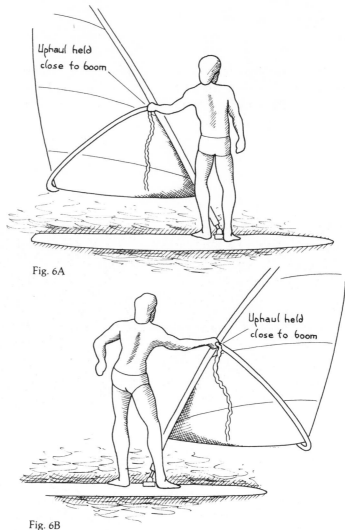

Uphaul held
close to boom

Fig. 6A

Uphaul held
close to boom

Fig. 6B

Lean the sail toward the bow and the board turns in one direction.
Lean it toward the back and the board turns the opposite way

Rapidly pull the line toward you, hand over hand, till the far end of the boom is completely out of the water. Hold the uphaul near the boom, allowing the sail to align itself downwind at right angles to the board, flapping loosely like a flag. Your back should be to the wind the whole time.

Later on, you'll gain enough experience to be able to lift the sail from the water at such an angle that the wind lifts it right into your hand.

ROPE TURNS
You can turn the board in one direction by tilting the sail toward the front, and in the other direction by tilting the sail aft (toward the back of the board). Figure 6 illustrates this.

Holding the uphaul close to the boom, arms outstretched so the far end of the boom is just above the water, lean the mast toward the front.

The front of the board turns away from the wind (bears off). Lean the mast toward the back and the bow turns the opposite way, toward the wind (heads up). At this stage don't worry whether you are "bearing off" or "heading up." Just concentrate on feeling the board turn one way then the other.

As the board turns keep your back to the wind and the sail in front of you by walking around the mast in small steps. Keep both feet close to the mast, so as not to tip the board. And try to keep those legs and hips from tensing!

Next, make full 360° turns in either direction as follows. Tilt the mast toward the front of the board and transfer your weight to the foot nearest the front to start the board turning. Walk around the mast, keeping the sail blowing straight out in front of your chest, your back always to the wind.

When the front of the board points directly downwind swing the sail over the front, then tilt your mast toward the back of the board so that the board keeps turning in the same direction.

Keep tilting the sail and walking around the universal till the board is back where it started, having turned through 360°.

Now turn the board through 360° in the opposite direction. Practice turning both ways till you do it easily.

Fig. 7A

Fig. 7B

Fig. 7C

Fig. 7D

Fig. 7E

Suzi Smyth demonstrates the basic rope turn

Fig. 7F

Fig. 8A
Align board at right angles to wind, sail downwind, your back to wind

Fig. 8B
Cross forward hand over back hand, and grasp boom near mast

THE START-UP SEQUENCE

To set sail you must perform a special start-up sequence. But before you sail off into the sunset bear in mind that a sailboat can sail at all orientations to the wind except directly toward the wind (upwind) and within 45° either side of directly upwind (see fig. 14). At first you'll drift downwind all too easily. To sail back to any point within 45° of directly upwind you'll have to take a zigzag course known as tacking (fig. 15).

Initially practice the start-up sequence on land by rigging the sail and putting the mast foot onto sand or grass. This removes the problem of balance so you can concentrate fully on the starting sequence, which must become smooth and automatic. If there's a simulator (device simulating turning motion of sailboard) available you can practice on a cut-down board. Otherwise mark front and back of an imaginary board on the ground at right angles to the wind.

The first step is to lift the sail from the water by following the instructions given in the beginning of this chapter. Then, keeping your feet on the board's centerline, move them to the sailing position you'll find easiest when new to the sport:

forward foot just beside and in front of the mast, back foot on about the center of the daggerboard. Now for the actual starting sequence:

1. Keeping your back to the wind, hold the uphaul and tilt the mast forward or back as necessary to align the board at a right angle to the wind, so you end up with the sail fluttering out downwind at right angles to the board.

2. Holding the uphaul with your back hand, cross your forward hand over the back hand to grasp the boom 6 to 10 inches from the mast. Keep the board at right angles to both wind and sail by tilting the mast forward or aft with your forward hand on the boom.

3. Pull the mast toward you with your forward hand and angle it slightly *toward the wind* and toward the bow, so the front of the boom is about a foot forward of your forward shoulder. Turn your body and forward foot slightly in the direction you'll be sailing, keeping your body upright, back straight and slightly hollow.

4. With your back hand grasp the boom slightly over shoulder width from your forward hand and pull the back of the sail toward you enough to fill it with wind. (This is called "sheeting in.") At the

Fig. 8C
Pull mast toward you and angle it forward (front of boom 1 foot ahead of forward shoulder) and slightly toward wind

Fig. 8D
Grasp boom with back hand and pull in back of sail enough to fill with wind. Tilt mast forward

Fig. 8E
When moving, bring mast back nearly to vertical

same time rake the mast slightly farther toward the front of the board. Keep that back straight and slightly hollow, and your bottom in!

5. As soon as you're moving bring the mast back almost to the vertical so you sail off in a more or less straight line. If you leave the mast angled forward too much the board will turn downwind.

CORRECT STANCE

In light wind the sailing stance is back straight, knees slightly bent and relaxed (fig. 9). As the wind gets stronger, lean back slightly to counter-balance its force on the sail. Your forward hand (mast hand) is near your forward shoulder and the forward arm is bent at the elbow. This arrangement allows you to rake the mast forward or back to steer. Later you will graduate to sailing with a straight forward arm, in the appropriate conditions, but at first you'll find keeping the forward arm slightly bent gives you more control.

Keep the mast vertical or, if the wind picks up, slightly to the same side of the board as you stand (to windward). Beginners often make the mistake of leaning the mast away from themselves (to

Fig. 9 *Correct stance*

leeward), which gives them less room for error, so that when a gust hits they are easily overpowered.

Glance at the sail to see that you pull it toward you with your back hand (sheet in) just enough to fill it with wind. Don't oversheet by pulling it toward you farther than necessary.

Avoid sailing with your torso bent forward. If a gust hits the sail pulling you forward, sheet out—that is, push the sail away from you with your back hand to relieve the pressure on the sail, still keeping the mast close to you with a bent forward arm. If you're being pulled hopelessly off balance, let go the boom with your back hand. Even let go with both hands and go for the uphaul until you've regained balance. If you can avoid dropping the sail in the water you'll save lots of hard work. Lifting the sail from the water repeatedly is what tires most beginners, and as you tire you learn less efficiently. So work on reacting quickly; then whenever that sail gets too much for you to hold, let go the boom and go for the uphaul rather than drop the sail in the water.

As your balance improves move your foot from the beginner's position to beside the mast step, turning it forward. This lets you drive the board forward from the hip with your front leg and, on a Windsurfer, prevents you from driving the front of the board under waves.

STEERING
You steer by raking the mast toward the front of the board or toward the back. Tilt the mast toward the front and the front turns downwind. Tilt the mast toward the back and you turn upwind. Raking the mast forward or back turns the sailboard because the wind makes the sail act like a lever, pivoting the hull about the daggerboard.

Get the feel of this by sailing an S-shaped course.

As you turn, the angle of the sail to the wind alters. So after turning downwind ease the sail out slightly with your back hand. And after turning upwind pull the sail in toward the board slightly with your back hand.

BASIC TACKING AND JIBING
Having learned to sail away from shore you'll find it useful to learn how to turn and sail back. The most basic form of turn is the rope turn. You simply stop sailing by transferring first your back hand and then your forward hand to the uphaul. And by leaning the mast toward the front or back of the board and pushing with your feet you turn the board through 180° while you step around the mast.

Sailors call a course change with the bow passing through the eye of the wind a "tack." (The eye

Fig. 10   *S-shaped course*

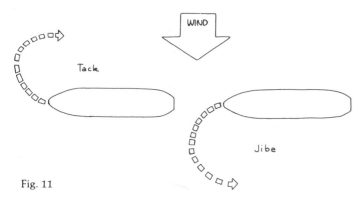

Fig. 11

of the wind is the direction from which the wind blows.) The opposite kind of turn, a course change with the stern passing through the eye of the wind, boardsailors call a "jibe."

As soon as you are able, begin practicing the following methods of tacking and jibing:

The tack

1. While sailing a straight course across the wind, tilt the mast aft until the end of the boom is almost touching the water. The board will start turning toward the wind.

2. When the bow points into the eye of the wind, the sail fluttering over the stern, transfer your back hand from the boom to the uphaul close to the mast. Step around the front of the mast, keeping close to the mast, also transferring your forward hand to the uphaul.

3. Tilting the mast away from you, swing the sail over the stern and step around the other side of the sail. Swing the sail out downwind to make a right angle with the board, which now points in the opposite direction to before the tack.

4. Execute the usual start-up routine.

Fig. 12A

Fig. 12B

Fig. 12C
Basic tack

Fig. 12D

Fig. 13A

Fig. 13B

Fig. 13C
Basic jibe

Fig. 13D

The jibe

In this maneuver you turn downwind, letting the sail swing across the front of the board as you stand facing forward, feet side by side either side of the daggerboard.

1. While sailing a straight course tilt the mast forward so you turn downwind.

2. As you turn so the bow points straight downwind, bring your forward foot back to beside the other, so you face the bow with a foot either side of the daggerboard, arms outstretched.

3. Transfer first your forward hand to the uphaul, then your back hand.

4. Let the sail swing across the front of the board.

5. Continue to swing the sail around till it is at right angles to the board, putting your new forward foot into the usual sailing position. (You can increase the rate of turn by leaning the sail forward and pulling it around with your new forward hand.) Sheet in to set sail.

CHOOSING YOUR COURSE

In keeping with the rest of this chapter, the information here is basic, intended for those new to sailing.

The diagrams show the various courses, named according to their orientation to the wind. Note that the angle of the sail to the wind changes very little, but that the angle the sail makes with the hull changes greatly.

Here are some tips on sailing various courses. Learn to be sensitive to the direction the wind is coming from. Bear in mind that as your sailing speed changes, the velocity and direction of the wind you actually feel will change, since the wind created by your forward motion interacts with the true wind.

Close reach

Beginners find a close reach an easy point of sail. Balance is easy, as is maintaining the course. Figure 14C shows the angle the sail makes to the

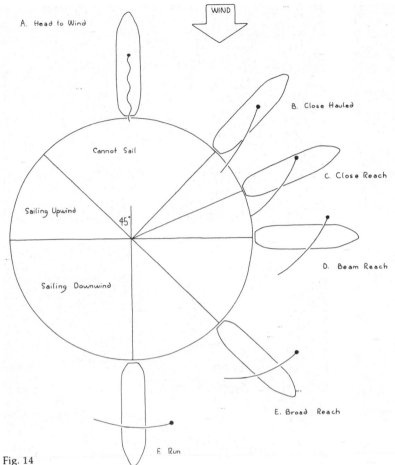

Fig. 14

Sail trim for various courses

A. Head to Wind

WIND

B. Close Hauled

Cannot Sail

C. Close Reach

Sailing Upwind

45°

D. Beam Reach

Sailing Downwind

E. Broad Reach

F. Run

Fig. 15

Tacking to a point upwind called "beating"

WIND

wind and to the board on a close reach. Practice this first. It's particularly valuable, since each time you fall you drift downwind, and this will enable you to gain ground upwind.

Beating to windward

Because it is impossible to sail directly into the wind you must gain ground upwind by "beating" —that is, by sailing upwind on alternate tacks (fig. 15). You progress most effectively upwind by sailing close-hauled. You'll sail relatively slowly on this course so sail patiently and carefully. Tack quickly and resume the close-hauled stance as soon as possible, or you'll drift downwind again.

Sailing close-hauled

Figure 17 shows the stance and sail position for sailing close-hauled (see fig. 14B). The mast must not lean to leeward (side of board away from wind). It is held close to the body. The ends of the

boom are over the downwind corner of the board.

If in this position the sail is luffing then you are too close to the wind, so bear off by tilting the mast forward slightly. (To determine whether your sail is luffing look at the forward third. If your sail is full of wind and curves smoothly from the mast to the back, or "leech," it is not luffing. If the front part is flapping and looks as if the wind is pushing it from the other side, it is luffing.)

When close-hauled you ought to be sailing so close to the wind that the sail is just short of luffing. Once you are sailing in this position test to make sure your sail is efficiently set by sheeting out till you see the sail luff. Then sheet in just enough to see and feel the wind fill the whole sail.

Sailing downwind

Sailing directly downwind is known as "running" (see figs. 14F, 18). To get onto a downwind course tilt your mast radically forward (booms 1 to 2 feet forward) and to windward, and sheet

Fig. 16   *Sail trim for close reach*

Fig. 17   *Sail trim for sailing close-hauled*

Fig. 18 *Sailing downwind*

out. The bow will turn downwind. Turn your body forward, shifting your feet so they are either side of the daggerboard well, one foot slightly ahead of the other for stability.

When pointing directly downwind sheet out fully, bringing the mast over to the windward side of the board so the sail is at right angles across the board. Look ahead through the window. Steer the board by tilting the sail to the right or left rather than fore and aft as you were doing on the close-hauled course. Sail tilted to the right makes the board turn left, and vice versa.

Balance is difficult in this position. Waves rock the board while your feet are off the centerline and you haven't got the sail to counterbalance you. If shaky, assume a lower stance—for example, drop down to one knee.

SAIL A CIRCULAR COURSE
Before you sail any distance from the shore use all you've learned by sailing around in circles.

Start off sailing a close reach. Head up to sail close-hauled. Tack quickly and smoothly by raking the sail back strongly till the end of the

boom touches the water, and get into the sailing position on the other side while the board still has headway.

Gradually bear off until you are running. Now jibe and return to the sailing position. Next circle in the opposite direction. When you can sail around in small circles extend these circles. Keep practicing different courses by selecting objects to sail toward, and practice your tacking till you tack smoothly and swiftly. Faster tacking methods are described in chapter 4.

GENERAL HINTS
During your first few hours windsurfing you may find these things useful to keep in mind:
• The wind may be rapidly changing direction and strength. If you're falling a lot this could be part of your problem. Avoid sailing downwind of tall buildings or other obstacles that cause air turbulence.
• You may be falling off forward because you aren't keeping your bottom in and leaning back with enough commitment. Lean back sufficiently

that if you misjudge, you fall backward into the water rather than forward. At this stage such a fall is a useful learning experience . . . next time you feel yourself falling back, be quicker to bend at the knees and simultaneously pull hard on the sail with your back hand to stop your fall.

• Anytime a gust pulls the sail to leeward and puts you off balance, luff the sail—that is, relieve the pressure by pushing the back of the sail away from you with your back hand, and pulling the mast toward you with your forward hand.

• If you are pulled forward at the waist by a small gust, it may help you recover if you bend at the knees and roll your bottom down and in toward the sail. Then lean back slightly, getting the strain into your thighs rather than your back, and straighten the forward leg (foot facing slightly forward) so that it pushes the board ahead when you sheet.

• Mimic closely the sail and body positions of experienced sailors. If you can, have friends sail alongside and copy them.

• Practice sail positions and maneuvers, such as tacking, on the beach by sticking the mast in the sand, holding the booms as if sailing. It may look comical, but you'll gain good experience and save many spills on the water.

• When you fall, stop and figure out why you fell and how to avoid it next time. If you don't know why you fell make a mental note to find out.

As you gain experience, these hints may help:
• Rather than simply leaning the mast toward

bow or stern to steer, you can steer more effectively by tilting the mast in the direction the front or back boom end points. To bear off, tilt the mast in the direction the front boom end points. To head up, tilt the mast toward the direction the back boom end points.

If you have difficulty picturing this, look at figure 8 (bearing off) in chapter 3, and imagine or draw a straight line joining the front and back ends of the booms. (The angle this line makes with your board depends on your point of sail, as shown by the sail trim diagrams in figure 14 of this chapter.) Extend the line beyond the front end of the booms; this line points about midway between the wind and the bow, and is the approximate direction you should tilt the mast toward in order to turn to a more downwind course. Conversely, extend the line beyond the back end of the booms; this is about the direction you tilt the mast to turn more toward the wind. This principle steers you for all courses, and has the virtue of making you sensitive to the fact that to maintain correct sail trim you sheet out slightly after bearing off, and sheet in slightly after heading up.

• As the wind increases and you lean back to counter it, *hang* your weight on the booms rather than pulling with tensed muscles.

• With increased wind you'll need to move your hands farther back on the booms to maintain control.

Chapter 4 discusses techniques for higher wind in more detail.

USEFUL INFORMATION

2

If you haven't sailed before, you'll find you've quite a lot to learn. Much of it you'll pick up simply by sailing and being around other sailors, so this chapter merely gives a few pointers.

SAIL ADJUSTMENT
Sail adjustment isn't critically important unless you are racing. When you are new to the sport you'll find that a fairly flat sail (clew pulled to within 2 to 3 inches of the boom end) allows you better control. Later apply this very approximate general rule: in lighter winds get maximum power by using a fuller sail, and as the wind strength increases put more tension on both the outhaul and downhaul.

A more detailed account of sail adjustment is given in chapter 10.

TAPING MAST BASES
If your mast base fits loosely into the hull, wrap tape around it so that it fits firmly in the slot. Don't make the fit so tight that you are liable to damage the hull (for example, cause delamination) when taking the mast base in and out. Use very sticky, broad, strong linen tape. Duct tape will do (though is a bit messy), and is available at most hardware stores.

GENERAL AWARENESS
On the water, since you are not a fish, you are in a somewhat foreign environment and not altogether in control of your destination . . . good reasons to be aware of potential hazards.

Currents can catch you unaware. In tidal waters you may set sail during slack tide (no current), then be carried out to sea when the ebb starts. Keep a constant check on reference points so that you notice if you drift from your launch site. Also watch for swirling and eddying water around a buoy; this can tell you whether there is a current, how strong it is and which direction it is flowing.

Weather can change suddenly for the worse. Check the weather report before you go out, and keep an eye on the sky while sailing. If a thunderstorm develops get to shore and away from that lightning rod we call a mast.

Miscellaneous hazards include fishing lines, powerboats, sailboat races, freighters, tugboats towing barges . . . and tidal waves.

Being alert to such things and in general being intelligently aware of your surroundings will greatly increase your chances of enjoying your sailboard for your normal lifespan.

RULES OF THE ROAD
All boats, especially those in crowded waterways, must abide by right-of-way rules.

Rule 1
There's a saying "Whether the stone hits the pitcher or the pitcher hits the stone, it won't go well for the pitcher." In other words, yours is probably the smallest boat in the water, and you are probably the least protected, so regardless of who has right-of-way, you'll come off worst in any collision. Hence rule 1: avoid collision and the risk of collision.

Rule 2

When two sailboats meet on opposite tacks, the one on port tack (booms to starboard) shall give way.

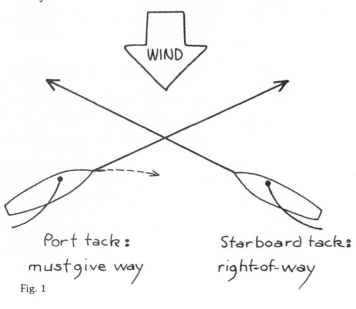

Port tack:
must give way

Starboard tack:
right-of-way

Fig. 1

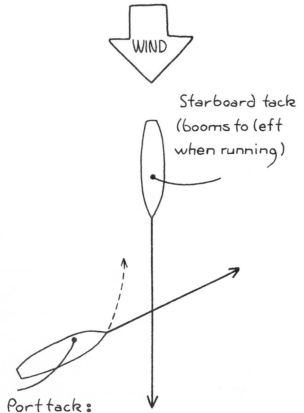

Starboard tack
(booms to left
when running)

Port tack:
must give way

Fig. 2

Rule 3

When two sailboats meet on the same tack, the boat to windward must give way.

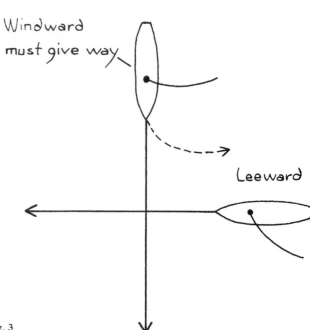

Windward
must give way

Leeward

Fig. 3

Rule 4

When one boat is overtaking another, the overtaking boat shall keep clear.

Rule 5

A boat that is obstructed by other right-of-way boats or by the shore may demand room to navigate around the obstruction.

Rule 6

When a sailboat and powerboat meet, the more maneuverable boat must give way—that is, don't demand rights from a supertanker.

You share the water with swimmers in addition to boats, so be especially careful to watch for them. If you run over someone you'll very likely cause serious injury.

USEFUL KNOTS

BOWLINE
TWO HALF HITCHES
PRUSIK HITCH
TRUCKER'S HITCH
CLOVE HITCH
OVERHAND
FIGURE EIGHT

Bowline
This knot is good for rigging various sailboards, and also for general use. The knot forms a loop that won't shrink, and never becomes difficult to untie.

Fig. 4

Two half hitches
Two half hitches will secure a line to almost anything.

Fig. 5

Roof Rack

Prusik hitch
Excellent for tying an inhaul to your mast.

Fig. 6A
Step one

Mast

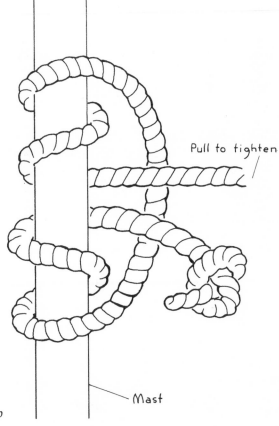

Pull to tighten

Fig. 6B
Step two

Mast

Trucker's hitch

This type of trucker's hitch is easy to tie, never difficult to untie, yet allows you to cinch down on your board as much as is necessary to keep it securely on your roof rack no matter how strong the wind.

Fig. 7A

Step one. Start by tying a slip knot about 10 inches from the roof rack

Fig. 7B

Step two. Next, loop your line under the roof rack, back up through the loop in your slip knot, and pull down hard to take up the slack

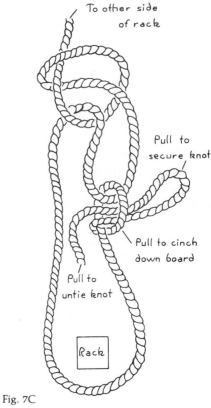

Fig. 7C

Step three. Finish off by tying a slip half hitch or two half hitches while still maintaining tension

Clove hitch

The clove hitch is useful for tying the inhaul to the mast, still better for tying harness lines to teak booms.

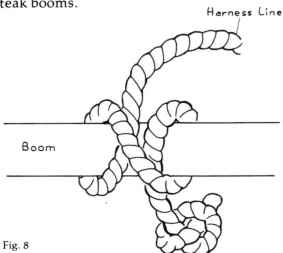

Fig. 8

Overhand

Can become impossible to untie.

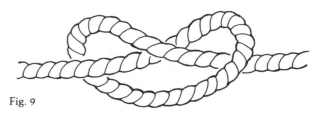

Fig. 9

Figure eight

Remains easy to untie.

Fig. 10

BASIC THEORY

3

Understanding some basic theory generally helps sailors learn more rapidly.

Your sail functions much like the wing of an airplane. Air flows over the surface of a wing and generates an upward force known as *lift*. Similarly, air flowing past your sail generates lift, but in a horizontal direction (fig. 1).

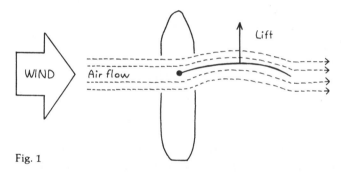

Fig. 1

Upon meeting the sail the air flow is separated to pass either side. The air flowing past the leeward side is accelerated by the sail's curve, causing a reduction of air pressure. The greater pressure on the windward side then pushes the sail toward this lower-pressure area of the leeward side—that is, it produces lift. The lift is generated roughly perpendicular to a line drawn from the mast to the clew (fig. 2).

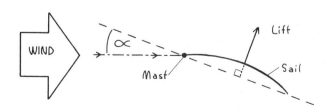

Fig. 2

To use your sail efficiently you must hold it at just the right angle (α) to the wind, this angle depending upon factors such as your point of sail. If the sail is held at too small an angle to the wind it luffs, and consequently part of its area is not being used to generate force (fig. 3).

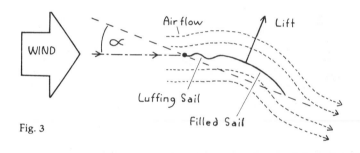

Fig. 3

If the sail is at too great an angle to the wind it stalls (fig. 4). The air can't flow smoothly past the leeward surface, but breaks up into swirls and eddies. There is no longer a reduction of pressure on the leeward side, so less overall driving force is generated. In fact, the wind merely pushes the sail along, just as it does when you run dead downwind.

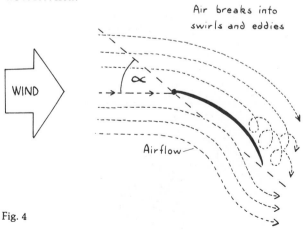

Fig. 4

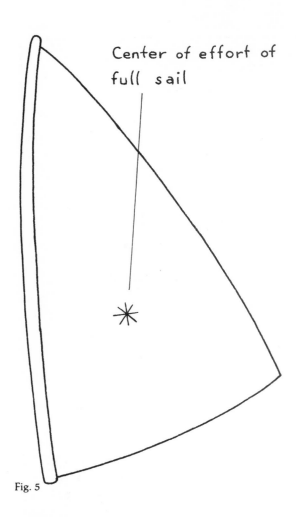

Center of effort of
full sail

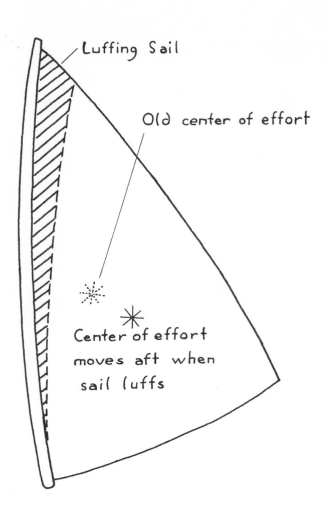

Luffing Sail

Old center of effort

Center of effort
moves aft when
sail luffs

Fig. 5

Between these two limiting angles of luff and stall there is a range of efficient sail lift generation. You can find this subject discussed in more detail in books on general sailing theory.

To improve your sailing ability you need to become sensitive to the balance of the boom in your hands. The center of effort (CE) of the sail is the point through which all the aerodynamic forces acting on the sail may be imagined to act. When a sail luffs a little, this CE moves aft (fig. 5) and puts more pressure on your back hand.

When the sail stalls the opposite happens: the CE moves forward, but in a far less pronounced way. Sensitivity to these variations will enable you to trim your sail more accurately and sail more efficiently.

DAGGERBOARD

Much of the force generated by the sail is in a sideways direction, particularly when close-hauled. Since we don't want to go sideways, we use a daggerboard. This is shaped to move through the water readily in a forward direction, but not easily in a sideways direction.

Just as the center of effort (CE) of a sail is the point through which you can imagine the forces on the sail to act, the center of resistance (CR) is the point through which you can imagine the resistance to motion to act.

When sailing close-hauled the CR is a point on the daggerboard through which sideways forces act to balance the sideways component of the forces acting through the CE.

STEERING

When we tilt the sail forward we move the CE ahead of the CR, so that the board bears off the wind. Similarly, when we tilt the sail back, we move the CE aft of the CR, so that the board heads up (fig. 6).

However, when you are running downwind the force on the sail is in a forward direction and the resistance is directly opposed to this force. To

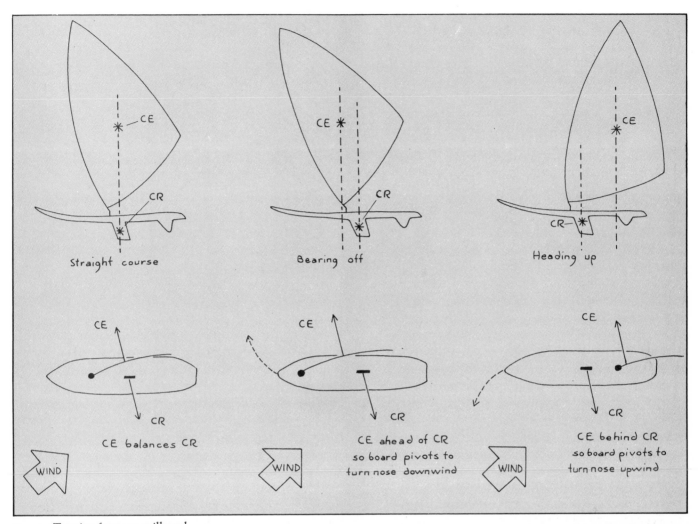

Fig. 6   *Turning forces on sailboard*

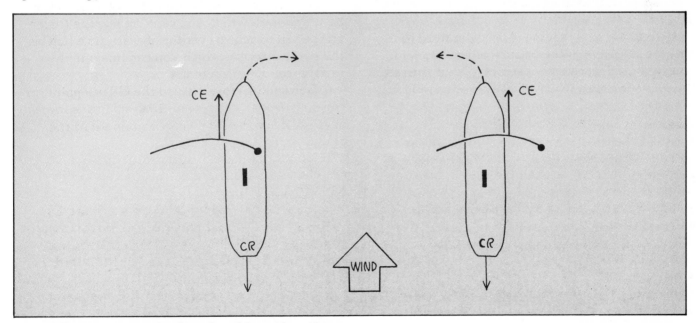

Fig. 7   *When running, steer by tilting the sail from side to side*

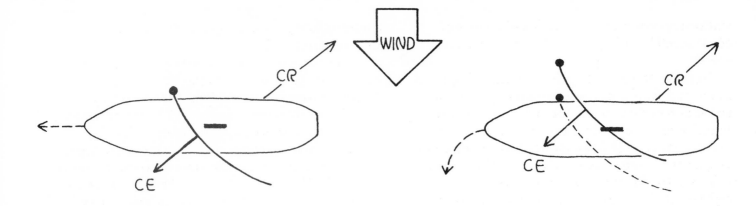

Fig. 8   Straight course   Bears off

steer, therefore, tilt the sail from side to side instead of forward and back (fig. 7).

From the previous two examples you can see why, when you are on a beam reach and wish to bear off to a broad reach, you tilt the sail slightly forward but mainly to windward (fig. 8).

STEERING BY SHEETING
As well as steering by tilting the sail, you can steer just by luffing or stalling. Remember that luffing the sail moves the CE aft. This means that you can head up by luffing, or bear off by stalling. It isn't a good idea to steer this way while racing, but an understanding of the principle is useful in boat handling and in stronger winds.

PLANING
Most sailboats move through the water. They push water aside as they pass. But some light-displacement boats, such as sailboards, are capable of skimming over the surface of the water—planing.

In light winds sailboards move at slower speeds and push through the water. But once the wind gets up to 10 to 12 knots they can go fast enough to rise to the surface of the water and plane. The difference in speed between planing and almost planing is surprisingly great; that's why your first success in 12 knots of wind is so exciting.

APPARENT WIND
The wind that is perceived by the sailor is known as the *apparent wind*. It is the vector combination of:

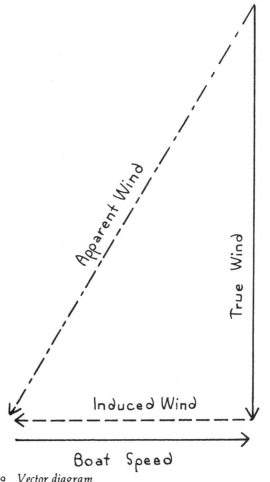

Fig. 9   *Vector diagram*

1. The *true wind* as observed by a stationary observer, and

2. The *induced wind* caused by the motion of the boat (which motion is also as perceived by a

stationary observer). This induced wind is of equal speed but of opposite direction to boat speed.

Consider the example of a true wind from the north at 8 mph, while you are sailing east at a speed of 6 mph: you will feel an apparent wind that is a vector combination of the true wind (8 mph, northerly) and the induced wind caused by your motion (6 mph, easterly). Substitute these values in the vector diagram and we have a right-angled triangle whose hypotenuse represents the value of the apparent wind. We can thus calculate the apparent wind as 10 mph from approximately the northeast.

In other words, in this example the wind to which you trim your sail when you start from a stationary position is the 8-mph wind from the north. You then accelerate to a steady-state speed of 6 mph, at which time your sail should be trimmed to the 10-mph apparent wind from approximately northeast.

It is the increase in the speed of the apparent wind that high-speed craft like iceboats, sand yachts, catamarans and sailboards use, at times, to go faster than the true wind. The faster they go, the stronger their apparent wind; the stronger their apparent wind, the faster they go. Of course, this progression doesn't go on forever: eventually the apparent wind is brought so close to head-on that the sail is unable to produce still more driving force.

Some iceboats can go more than four times the speed of the wind because of the very low drag of the runners on ice. At the time of writing, sailboards have been officially timed at nearly 1¼ times the speed of the wind. However, you'll find that the only time you really notice your apparent wind is when surfing waves (chapt. 11).

Ken Winner wave jumping at Zeros, a southern California surf spot

STRONGER WINDS

4

THE 8-KNOT BARRIER

Your technique and confidence have improved sufficiently that you feel ready to tackle higher winds. So one day when the wind picks up to 8 to 10 knots you rig your board and get out onto the water . . . only to discover you seem to be back to square one.

Each time you lift the sail you take a ducking. Either you take a catapult fall off frontward or, most likely, every time you sheet in, the board stubbornly turns to face the wind and you fall off backward. This is the 8-knot barrier. But in fact the technique required to pass it isn't hard to master.

PRECAUTIONS

Use good sense when you go out in windier conditions than you've encountered before. Think of the worst things that could happen, and take steps to avoid these things.

Don't go out in the Atlantic Ocean with the wind blowing toward Bermuda; you'll be blown away. Go with a friend, preferably a competent sailor. Don't choose a place with two meters of chop; you'll fall too often. And if there's the slightest risk of being cold, wear a wet suit.

STARTING UP

This is the hard part. In stronger wind your start differs from the start you learned earlier in two main aspects: before you sheet in, you tilt the mast across the board to windward; and you actually fall back toward the water before pulling in with your back hand.

However, first you have to pull the sail out of the water without getting a hernia. Keep your knees bent, your back straight, and lean back using your God-given weight and your thigh muscles to haul that sail up. Get it up quickly and keep it completely out of the water. If the clew dips in, the wind may fill the sail and pull it out of your hands.

Prepare to sheet in—this is the really hard part. Aim your board so you're headed on a close reach, as balance is easiest on this heading. Now reach over to the boom with your mast hand, as usual, and tilt the mast forward and well to windward. This is a key move. Study the first frame of figure 1 and notice the position of the mast: forward and well to windward.

Your forward foot mustn't be too far forward or you may find your sailboard driven nose under water like a sounding whale. Front foot alongside the mast, feet widely spaced, is a good position.

Next, grab the boom with your sheet hand, sail still luffing. Fall back toward the water and then sheet in. People have performed great acts of faith: they've built monumental cathedrals; they've died for their beliefs; now they must fall back *before* they sheet in.

If you sheet in too much you'll be pulled forward into the water; if you don't sheet in enough you'll fall backward into the water. Regard your wettings as baptism into the brotherhood of boardsailors. Strive on undaunted. And eventually you'll lean back just the right amount, sheet in just the right amount, and sail away with your faith confirmed.

Don't let your waist bend. Rather, try to fill the sail a little while keeping it tilted forward and to windward, and start the board moving slowly by letting your straight front leg drive it forward. If you're being pulled forward on sheeting in, luff the sail to reduce its pull. Make sure you're

Fig. 1A *Tilt luffing sail*

Fig. 1B *Lean back before sheeting*

Fig. 1C *Sheeted in and sailing*

headed on a close reach, and fall back again. Drop your body back in gradual stages to fill the sail a little more, until you are able to fill it completely and go full speed.

At first don't worry too much about your stance. But as you gain confidence aim for the stance shown in figure 2. Get your back straight first, then worry about moving your hands closer to the balance point of the boom, so you feel equal force on either hand. Hang your weight on the boom, to counter this force. Then, when you are in better control of the sail and are using it to maintain your balance, get your feet closer together.

Fig. 2 *Stronger wind sailing stance*

CHOPPY WATER

Choppy water demands you set sail quickly and tack smoothly. Don't stand struggling for the perfect start-up position before sheeting in. As long as your sail is luffing you are vulnerable to even the smallest of waves. But with the stabilizing influence of a full sail in your hands you can sail through anything.

When you are tacking concentrate on getting to the other side of the sail rapidly, so that if you start to fall backward all you have to do is pull in with your back hand.

BEARING OFF

As the wind increases, bearing off becomes difficult. You need to tilt the sail forward to bear off, but you need to get your weight back to counter the sail's pull. Since you can't increase your arm length by 2 feet you'll have to try an alternative.

The real knack to bearing off is the same as for getting started. What you do is crouch down a little, maintaining good sail trim (don't luff or stall), and tilt the sail to windward.

It's very likely you'll be catapulted the first few times you try this maneuver. The sail will suddenly pull very strongly. You'll pull back, but the sail will be stronger, and you'll find yourself in the water in front of the board.

Avoiding a catapult can be easier if you sheet the sail in and out, rapidly and repeatedly, just a bit, as you are bearing off. This prevents you committing the sail to a setting that will lead to a fall. It makes you more sensitive to the trim that will work best, and makes your acceleration slower and therefore easier to deal with.

DAGGERBOARD PLANE

While reaching in winds of 12 to 15 knots you'll find the board rolls from side to side under your feet, or turns completely on edge, dumping you off. This is caused by daggerboard plane. Your daggerboard is generating so much lift that it rises to the surface of the water, forcing the board onto its rail.

Daggerboard plane can get so severe even at moderate speeds that the board oscillates from rail to rail. One solution is to pull your daggerboard up halfway. To do this, luff on a beam reach heading. Hold the boom with the mast held forward and to weather to maintain heading.

Fig. 3A

Fig. 3B *Bearing off. Notice sail tilted to windward rather than just forward*

Then reach down quickly with your sail hand and pull the daggerboard up halfway. Quickly set sail again. You'll be able to sail satisfactorily as long as it isn't too windy and your course isn't too broad.

However, since the daggerboard now fits very loosely in its well it can angle one way and another, changing its angle of attack and making the board once again unmanageable if the wind is very strong.

The solution is then to pull out the daggerboard entirely and hang it on your arm. Follow the procedure for pulling it halfway, pulling it right out instead. To get going again head the board to below a beam reach by tilting your luffing sail forward. Lean back, sheet in, and concentrate on driving the bow off the wind with your forward foot. It is difficult to get bearing off and going, so if you find yourself heading up or sliding sideways, stop. Tilt your sail forward and start again on a heading just below beam reach.

Other solutions to the problem of daggerboard plane depend upon the particular type of sailboard you have. If you have a Mistral, for example, you need only swing the daggerboard back till parallel with the hull and it will no longer try to turn the hull over. Special daggerboards, discussed in chapter 6, are also used to control this problem.

HINTS TO KEEP IN MIND

1. At first you may find that another way to help stop your sailboard from stubbornly turning its nose into the wind in those critical seconds after sheeting in is to physically lever it away by pushing out with the front leg and pulling in with the back leg. This technique you'll use less as you get better. You'll rely more on placing your weight in the right place, and having better balance, to make the board bear off.

2. When you first try to get going in stronger winds you may not be leaning out enough, so visualize yourself playing tug-of-war with the booms.

3. Shoes can help give traction at this point, but they reduce your feel for the board. Without shoes you have to be more sensitive in sail control

Fig. 4A   *Faster tacking. Method 1*

Fig. 4B

Fig. 4C

Fig. 4D

to avoid slipping. Hence the handicap of poor traction can make you a better sailor. If you are slipping, put more of your weight on the boom. This transfers driving force to the mast and off your feet.

4. In gusty winds, if a lull hits, crouch immediately to avoid falling backward. In a very severe lull you can even hold the mast down low with your mast hand, to crouch even lower, thus maximizing the righting moment of the sail on your body.

FASTER TACKING

To go with your newfound prowess in windy conditions you'll need faster methods of tacking. It is especially important that when you get into rougher conditions you are able to tack quickly, otherwise you are left at the mercy of unexpected waves without the steadying influence of a full sail.

Method 1 (Fig. 4)

1. Lean the sail strongly back to head into the wind on starboard tack. As the bow crosses the eye of the wind, move your right foot forward and to leeward, and your right hand to the mast just below the booms.

2. Pass in front of the mast, placing your left foot in front of the mast step; grasp the mast below the booms with your left hand and let go with your right hand.

3. Step back with your right foot as you tilt the mast forward with your left hand and grasp the boom with your right hand.

4. Grasp the boom with your left hand, step back a little with your left foot and sheet in.

Two other methods of tacking that are very similar involve a little less hand motion:

Method 2 (Fig. 5)

Instead of grasping the mast with first your forward hand and then your back hand, reach directly to the mast with your back hand. Then complete the tack with steps 3 and 4 of method 1.

Method 3 (Fig. 6)

Instead of going for the mast with either hand, just slide your back hand forward on the boom as you let go the forward hand. The actions are the same as in method 2 except that you are saving the extra motion of grabbing the mast.

The first method is the most serviceable for all conditions, especially when you don't want to mess up. Holding the mast with both hands gives you a lot of support—and it's easy to find the mast when you need it.

Regardless of which method you choose, the most important thing in tacking well is making sure you practice a lot, go slowly at first and do exactly the same move each time.

Fig. 5 *Method 2. Photo illustrates differences from method 1*

Fig. 6 *Method 3. Photo illustrates difference from method 2*

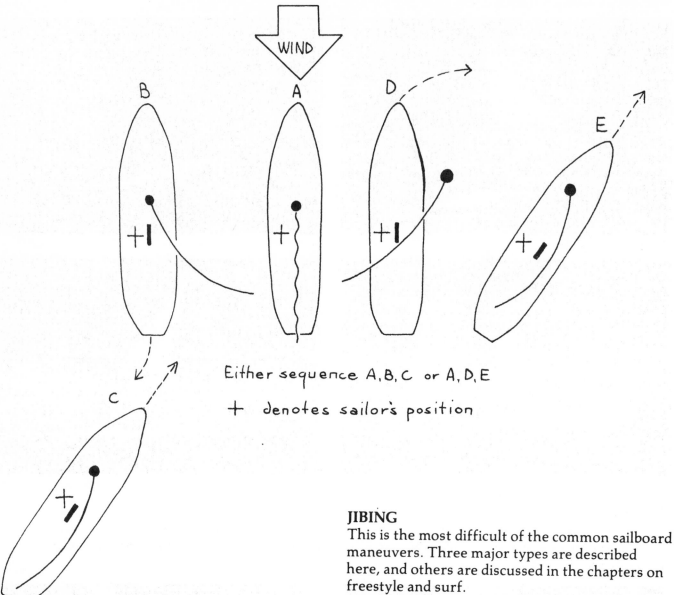

Either sequence A,B,C or A,D,E

+ denotes sailor's position

Fig. 7   *Heading off on port tack*

However, you may find as you complete your tack that you aren't headed off in the other direction as the book promised you'd be. Instead you are still headed directly into the wind. Don't panic. Just tilt the sail well forward, lean back and sheet in strongly (fig. 7). You'll head off on your new tack immediately—provided you don't fall in the water first.

Another way of gaining your balance and bearing off from head to wind after a tack is to tilt your mast aft and sheet out until the sail is partially filled from the back. Your board will turn to its proper heading, then you can sheet in and go (fig. 7).

JIBING
This is the most difficult of the common sailboard maneuvers. Three major types are described here, and others are discussed in the chapters on freestyle and surf.

Running jibe
1. Bear off the wind on starboard tack as you did for your rope jibe.
2. Continue bearing off until the stern of the board has passed through the eye of the wind. Then, keeping the mast well aft, transfer your left hand to the mast and release the boom with your right hand.
3. As the sail swings around, grasp the boom with your right hand, then with your left, and sheet in on your new tack.

You can do very sharp, quick jibes this way, but only with a lot of wind, special daggerboard and skeg (chapt. 6) and months or even years of practice.

Fig. 8A *Running jibe*

Fig. 8B

Fig. 8C

Fig. 8D

Push jibe

1. Bear off as for the running jibe, but before you are headed dead downwind, back the sail (fill the sail from the back).

2. Push on it gently, don't force it, as the board turns. When you are ready, sheet in and go.

Fig. 9A *Push jibe*

Fig. 9B

Fig. 10A *Power jibe*

Fig. 10B

Fig. 10C

Fig. 10D

Power jibe

This is difficult but excellent for changing direction quickly.

1. Reaching on starboard tack, step forward, transfer your left hand (back hand) from the boom to the mast and release the boom with your right hand.

2. Pause to steady yourself and to allow the board to slow down. Then grab the other boom with your right hand well back from the mast and back the sail.

3. Pull with your right hand and kick the board around to port tack.

HEAVY AIR (force 5 to 6)

The force that the wind exerts increases as the square of its velocity. The difficulty you'll have controlling your board increases at about the same rate, so by the time you can handle a standard rig such as the Windsurfer or Windglider in forces 5 and 6 you can consider yourself a good sailor by any standards.

Upwind

Sailing upwind in heavy air is tricky. When you first get going, you're faced with the problem of where to put your hands. Since in heavy air thirty to fifty percent of the sail will be luffing, the center of effort of the sail is farther aft than normal. Hence your hands should go much farther aft. Place them about 2 feet apart and far enough back that there is about the same amount of pull on each.

Next, you have to think about where to put your feet. Since you are going pretty fast, even upwind, and since much of your weight is on the booms rather than on the board, you'll encounter the problem of daggerboard plane. The board will want to stand up on its leeward rail. To counter this, put your feet as far out on the windward rail as possible.

But just standing on the rail isn't always enough to keep it down. Every time you lean out more, sheet in more and put more weight on the booms, you put less weight on the rail, allowing it to rise again. To sail well to windward you have to sheet in enough to bring your board to the verge of railing, but no more. The amount that you lean out and sheet in depends on your weight. Heavier people can sheet in more and go faster before the board starts to rail up, so it's less of a problem for them.

The next problem to confront you is fatigue. This usually waits till you're a good distance from shore before it makes an appearance. Fight fatigue by being relaxed. Sail with arms straight and shoulders loose; your arms should be like cables from which your body is suspended. Then when a good gust hits, tries to pull you over and makes the board head up, simply twist your body so that the sail luffs a little more and tilts forward a little more. When the gust eases, twist your body back so that the sail fills a bit more and tilts aft again. If you don't tilt the sail forward when you luff, you'll head up; then the wind will hit the other side of your sail and slam you into the water. If, on the other hand, you don't luff but rather try to lean out and sheet in, either you'll be unsuccessful and head up anyway, or you'll be successful and the board will start to rail up. In both cases you'll be expending more energy than necessary.

Off the wind

Off the wind you'll need to pull your daggerboard out, even if it's the type that swings back parallel to the hull. In the lulls you'll find water spurts from the daggerboard well. If it's hitting you in the face, block the well with your foot. In the gusts you'll be going so fast that the board scarcely touches the water and no geysers shoot through the well. Windsurfer sailors call that "skipping."

Whereas at slower speeds you'll want to be forward on the board for maximum speed, at skipping speeds you'll move as far back as possible.

Equally, at slower speeds you can bury the windward rail a little in order to head upwind. But at skipping speeds you'll do better to keep the board flat or tilted slightly to leeward in order to head up a little. If you're going fast enough to skip, be prepared to bounce when you fall.

Jibing

To jibe at high speed with your daggerboard out, crouch down, bear off and step aft as far as you can without sinking the tail so much that you slow down. Continue bearing off until your stern is well past the eye of the wind. Change your foot position for the new tack and swing the sail around. Keep the mast tilted way aft during this entire maneuver.

ATTIRE

5

HYPOTHERMIA

Hypothermia—a lowered deep body temperature—is one of the boardsailor's most dangerous enemies. Falls into cold water and exposure to chill winds can rapidly lower your body temperature, and as mentioned in chapter 1, prolonged immersion in water as warm as 20°C. (68°F.) can cause loss of consciousness. Already hypothermia has claimed the life of one boardsailor. Bear this in mind, and if you are out sailing and find yourself shivering uncontrollably, go to shore and warm up before your body temperature drops to a point where heat loss becomes difficult to reverse without medical attention.

This chapter on attire is devoted to reducing the danger, but you'll do well to read a more thorough discussion of the subject early on in your windsurfing career.

When deciding what to wear on the water, ask yourself the following questions:

- Can I possibly be stuck out on the water for several hours
- Am I likely to fall in a lot
- What is the water temperature
- What is the air temperature
- What is the windchill factor
- Is the sun likely to stay out

THE BEST COMPROMISE

The best wet suit for most conditions is the ⅛-inch long-john type. This keeps cold water off your legs yet leaves your arms free to move. If it's too cold for just a long john, the addition of a light jacket will usually do.

WINTER WEAR

If you sail when the air temperature is under –10°C. (15°F.), you need a psychiatrist more than you need a wet suit. When the air is –10°C. to +7°C. (15°F. to 45°F.), the water –1°C. (30°F.) and the wind 15 to 25 knots, you need boots, gloves, a diver's hood, pants and jacket.

Boots: cold-weather boots should be durable, insulated rubber, with nonskid soles. There are adequate sailing boots of this sort in shops that cater to dinghy sailors. Shoes designed especially for boardsailors are widely available in Europe and increasingly available in North America.

Gloves: in very cold weather you can use three-fingered gloves of ¼-inch or 3/16-inch neoprene, covered on both sides with nylon. However, with these you need a harness to enable you to hang onto the booms.

Hood: a diver's hood keeps your head warm and helps keep cold water from running down your neck.

Pants and jacket: you need ¼-inch to 3/16-inch neoprene over the rest of your body. It should be a snug fit, except around the arms and shoulders where you need freedom of movement. For a good fit in that area you'll need a tailored jacket.

WARMER CONDITIONS

As things warm up you can start casting off your bonds. The hood is first to go. Granted, a lot of heat is lost from the head, but the hood prevents you feeling the wind and impedes hearing. A knitted woolen cap or toque is a good alternative.

Once the air and water are over about 10°C. (50°F.), start to think about leaving off your gloves and boots.

In 10°C. to 15°C. (50°F. to 60°F.) weather, ⅛-inch neoprene is all you need. Here the long-john suit with a tailored ⅛-inch long-sleeve top to go with it is a warm, comfortable combination. Useful in these conditions is an excellent "Breeze-breaker" made by O'Neill, with wet-suit torso and thick fabric sleeves. As the temperature rises over 15°C. the neoprene top can be replaced by a sweater, flannel shirt or Windbreaker.

On windy, cloudy days in the tropics a neoprene vest will do. On the sunny days not even a swim-suit is essential.

BUYING THE WET SUIT

Though the most expensive wet suit is not necessarily the best, the cheapest is unlikely to be a good buy, either for warmth or for long wear.

Wet suits are made from neoprene with a lining of synthetic cloth for strength. They have either a lining on the inside or a lining both inside and out.

A suit with just a lining inside allows you to regain your ideal body temperature after a fall more quickly than a double-lined suit, because the outside lining absorbs water, which then takes up heat as it evaporates in the wind. However, single-lined wet suits tear and wear out more easily. A good compromise is a suit with part single, part double lining. An outside lining on parts that take a beating—knees, elbows, seat and cuffs—makes for a longer-lasting suit.

Plastic zippers near the ankles are worth the extra money. Without them you'll get so frustrated trying to get the suit past your heels that you'll feel like chewing it off.

HIGH FASHION

Do you ever find yourself preparing to go wind-surfing only to open your closet and find you haven't a *thing* to wear? If so, you'll be thrilled to discover that fashion designers are finally recognizing the sailor's need for style and sex appeal.

Imported from Germany's house of Mistral comes a *stunning* collection in blue, red and white of body-hugging rubber suits, designed to strike envy right down to the skeg of every other sailor.

Mistral suits come in full body, long john and (for the more daring) shortie styles, all aimed at warming up those windy days on the water. Top-of-the-line suits even have a racing stripe. *Zehr chic.*

SPECIAL EQUIPMENT

6

Special equipment—that is, equipment that doesn't come as standard on most sailboards—can help you handle heavy air and rough water. It can also increase your enjoyment of the sport regardless of conditions.

SAILS

Tiny sails in the range of 25 to 30 square feet (2.3 to 2.8 square meters) are used for teaching. They are produced by various manufacturers, both for standard rigs and for shortened masts and booms.

Sails between 40 and 55 square feet (3.7 to 5.1 square meters) are also used for beginners. In winds over about 20 knots (depending on the sailor's weight) experts use 40- to 55-square-foot sails, too.

Sails in the standard size range, about 58 to 68 square feet (5.4 to 6.3 square meters), are suitable for winds from 3 to 20 knots. The Windsurfer sail, incidentally, is measured by sailmakers at about 61 square feet (5.7 square meters). Most European boards have sails of about 65 square feet (6 square meters).

There are, of course, much larger sails available to those sailors big in pocket but short on wind. These allow you to go a bit faster in light air, but are mainly notable·for giving the sensation of hanging onto a parachute.

Sails without battens are popular for daily recreational use, for high wind and for surf. Battens tend to get broken or lost, and there's no good way to furl a sail with the battens in.

More sophisticated sails are discussed in a later chapter.

Reefing sails

Another valuable sail is the reefing sail, a sail that you can reduce in size without taking a knife to. The quickest, most popular type incorporates a zipper (fig. 1) which, when undone, removes 10 to 15 square feet (0.9 to 1.4 square meter) of sail area.

A good sailmaker can make such a sail so well that the shape is not too badly affected by the presence of the zipper. Once the excess material has been removed it can go into your harness pouch.

Battens

Because ordinary battens tend to break, especially in surf, some Hawaiians* started using battens made of Lexan, a polycarbonate product. A Lexan batten is stiff enough to hold out the roach of a sail, but flexible enough to be tied in a knot. You can obtain Lexan by looking in the yellow pages under "Plastics." You'll find that most suppliers of Plexiglas also have Lexan, and they'll cut it to the sizes you specify.

---

*"Hawaiians" as used throughout the text refers to various windsurfing enthusiasts resident in Hawaii, including Larry Stanley, Mike Horgan, Pat Love, Ken Kleid, Dennis Davidson, Andy Chaffee and Colin Perry.

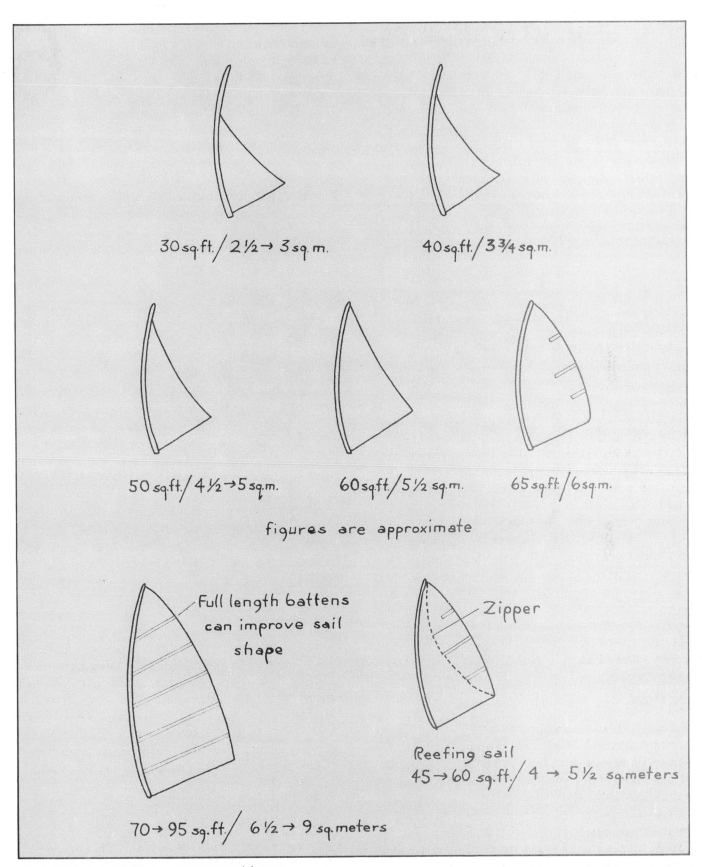

30 sq.ft. / 2½ → 3 sq.m.   40 sq.ft. / 3¾ sq.m.

50 sq.ft. / 4½ → 5 sq.m.   60 sq.ft. / 5½ sq.m.   65 sq.ft. / 6 sq.m.

figures are approximate

Full length battens
can improve sail
shape

Zipper

Reefing sail
45 → 60 sq.ft. / 4 → 5½ sq.meters

70 → 95 sq.ft. / 6½ → 9 sq.meters

Fig. 1   *Sails are available in various sizes and designs*

Mast extension

Large sails require an extension to the foot of the mast. You can make one fairly easily (fig. 2). An extension fabricated of three pieces of 6061-T6 aluminum is light, strong and durable. Look in your local yellow pages under "Aluminum" and find a tubing supplier. Tubing with a wall thickness of about $\frac{1}{16}$ inch is suitable. You'll have to work out the other dimensions as these depend upon your mast and sail, but general guidelines follow.

The three pieces that make up the extension should telescope snugly. Part A should fit snugly about 6 inches into the mast and about 2 inches into part B. Part C, which fits around the top of B to form the shelf that the mast sits upon, should be about 2 inches long. The length of B then depends upon how much you need to extend your mast. To hold the assembly together use four aluminum rivets, $\frac{3}{16}$ inch in diameter by $\frac{3}{8}$ inch long.

Windows

If you plan to do some sailing in breaking waves, or if you just like to avoid running into things, you'll find it useful to have big windows in your sail. Figure 3 shows a popular arrangement.

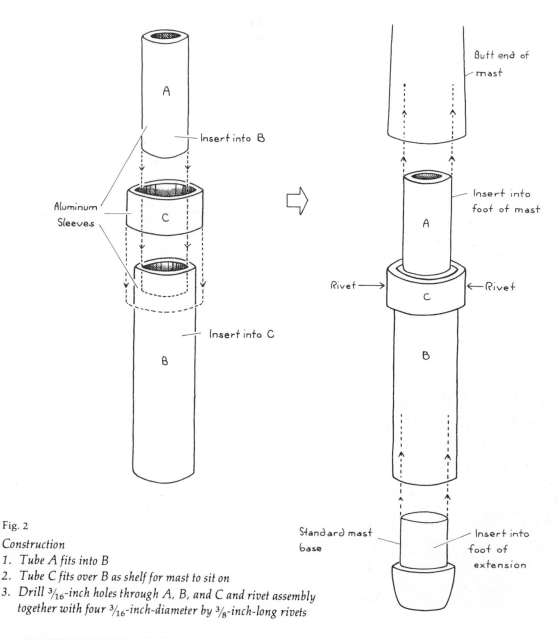

Fig. 2

Construction

1. *Tube A fits into B*
2. *Tube C fits over B as shelf for mast to sit on*
3. *Drill $\frac{3}{16}$-inch holes through A, B, and C and rivet assembly together with four $\frac{3}{16}$-inch-diameter by $\frac{3}{8}$-inch-long rivets*

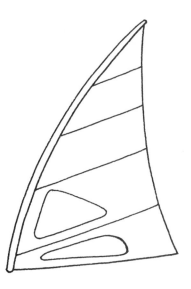

Fig. 3   *A useful arrangement of sail windows*

DAGGERBOARDS

Some sailboards have daggerboards that are suitable for a wide variety of conditions. The daggerboards on most of the popular European boards, for example, the German-made "Sailboard," swing to the positions illustrated (fig. 4).

Such an arrangement is adequate for low-key recreational sailing in light to moderate winds,

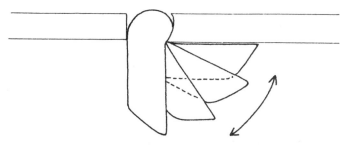

Fig. 4   *Variable-position daggerboard*

Fig. 5
Full-size Windsurfer daggerboard (left) next to a high-wind Windsurfer daggerboard, both shown at angle of use

but not for getting the best performance possible in high winds and/or waves.

For high-wind sailing on Windsurfer, Mistral and Windglider boards, the daggerboard on the right in figure 5 works well. It moves the center of lateral resistance aft to lessen the heading-up tendency, reduces the total area to reduce the daggerboard's tendency to plane, and has a swept-back leading edge that also reduces daggerboard plane. This design was developed by various Hawaiians.

A slightly more versatile daggerboard is shown on the left in figure 6, in the down position. Down it allows for good windward performance, and when swung back up a few degrees it permits high-speed reaching. The first design of this general type was by the Charchulla brothers.

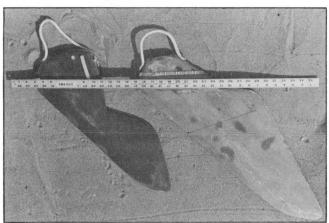

Fig. 6
Adjustable high-wind daggerboard (left) in down position and freestyle daggerboard

Skegs

The relationship between daggerboard size and skeg size determines how quickly a given board turns. A big skeg with small daggerboard makes for slow turning, whereas a large daggerboard with small skeg allows quick turning. Of course, the stronger the wind the more quickly you turn, whatever the skeg-daggerboard setup.

Table 1 shows nine combinations of daggerboard and skeg and gives a rough idea of what they are good for. Since most manufacturers don't offer a variety of skeg sizes, you'll have to make smaller ones yourself. Just cutting down a stock skeg is usually adequate.

Daggerboards \ Skegs	Big	Medium	Small
Big	Triangle Racing	Light Air Racing	Light Air Freestyle
Medium	Moderate Air Racing	Moderate Air Freestyle	Light – Moderate Air Freestyle
Small	Heavy Air Waves & Racing	Heavy Air Waves & Freestyle	Moderate Air Waves & Freestyle

Table 1

LEASH

If you go out in strong winds you are foolish not to have a strong leash connecting your rig to your hull. Should the hull and rig become separated the hull may drift faster than you can swim. A piece of line screwed to a threaded insert in your board (or attached by fiberglass to your board) and looped around the universal will work on boards that don't come equipped with a leash.

BUNGEED UPHAUL

Another innovation from Hawaii, the bungeed uphaul is a simple, elegant solution to the problem of runaway rope. There are no loose ends flailing about and the uphaul is always there. when you need it, neatly alongside the mast.

To make a bungeed uphaul get yourself 9 feet of line (½-inch Sampson Blue Streak or similar), 6 feet of ¼-inch shock cord, and a plastic hook of the sort illustrated (fig. 7).

1. Burn each end of the ½-inch Sampson Blue Streak.

2. Tie the hook onto the end of the shock cord with an overhand knot.

3. Work the shock cord into the line the way you put a drawstring into a swimsuit.

4. The 9 feet of line is now crammed onto 6 feet of shock cord. Slip the end without the hook on it through the hole in your boom end and tie a figure-eight knot in the end.

5. To adjust the uphaul to the height of your booms, and keep it taut and close to the mast, pull some of the shock cord out at the hook end and retie the overhand knot.

HARNESS

Developed by the Charchulla brothers of Germany, and independently by the Hawaiians, the harness gained acceptance gradually between 1975 and 1979. It became legal for racing in two of the three IWCA regions in 1979 and has now gained the acceptance of Windsurfer sailors worldwide, though sailors of other boards, mainly in Europe, are lagging behind.

The benefits of a harness are immense. You can actually enjoy four hours of high-wind sailing, and you can cruise long distances in enough wind to make it interesting. Race courses can be longer, more on the order of a normal yacht-racing course. And hands no longer need be like leather.

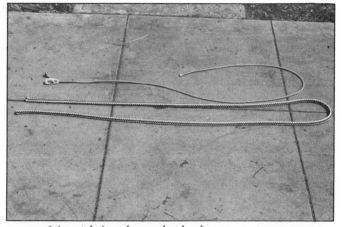

Fig. 7A *Materials for a bungeed uphaul*

Fig. 7B *Completed uphaul*

Fig. 8 *Hawaiian harness in use*

Different harnesses

The basic Hawaiian harness, first introduced to the international boardsailing public at the 1976 Windsurfing World Championships, is the most popular. It consists of a padded sling that holds a large hook in front of the chest (fig. 8).

A variation of the Hawaiian harness is made by Platt Johnson of Newport, Rhode Island. Platt's harness has thick padding for comfort and flotation and is designed to provide support for the lower back. It really is much more comfortable for cruising than the smaller type.

There are other harnesses available, with hooks nearer the pelvis, hooks that go directly to the boom, cam cleats on the booms, etc.

Harness lines

The Hawaiian harness requires harness lines. These should be ¼-inch or ⁵⁄₁₆-inch braided prestretched Marlow. Tie them onto wooden booms with a clove hitch. With this knot the line can easily be slid up or down the boom as needed, but will otherwise stay put.

Attaching lines to aluminum booms is more difficult because the covering over the aluminum usually impedes sliding of the line. One way to overcome this difficulty is to make four straps, each 1 inch wide by 5 inches long, with a ¼-inch or ⁵⁄₁₆-inch grommet (depending on your line) in each end as in figure 9. In fact, a sailmaker will usually make these straps for you, and they'll be stronger than ones you make yourself.

Arrange on the booms as illustrated. With

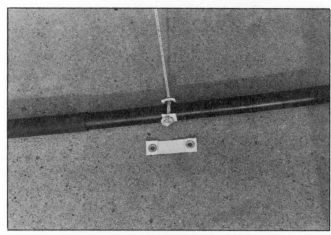

Fig. 9 *Strap attaches harness line to boom*

tension on the line the straps won't budge; in fact, they won't move unless you loosen them with a flip of the thumb and then slide them.

If you prefer to have the ends of your harness lines stationary, you can buy the type of strap designed in Hawaii and available from many sailboard dealers.

If you tie the line onto the boom, use 5 to 6 feet of line. The strap method requires only 3 to 4 feet of line. Try the ends about 18 inches apart with about 10 inches of slack between line and boom. (Some like as much as 4 feet between the ends; these people don't need to slide the line, but need more of it.) People with shorter arms will find less slack more suitable.

Hook position
The hook can be positioned with the open end up or down. With the open end down, hooking in is easier, but unhooking rapidly to avoid being pulled forward into a bad fall is difficult. For this reason many prefer the open end up, and the technique below is described for that orientation.

Learning to use the harness
Don't try the harness until you can tack and jibe in 12-knot winds. Then select a day with 8- to 12-knot steady wind, and find flat water.

1. Sail on a close reach and notice where your hands are comfortable. Position the line between them, each end the same distance from the nearer hand. There should be about 10 inches of slack in the line.

2. Hook in while sailing on a close reach by lifting the boom and pulling it toward you, allowing the line to fall into the hook.

3. Gradually allow the line to hold more of your weight. Continue close reaching for a while, so you can luff easily and avoid falls.

4. Practice hooking and unhooking quickly. To unhook pull the booms toward you, lift and push away. If you are about to be pulled over, pull the booms toward you, bend your knees and waist and let go the booms; the rig will fall but you won't. (This only works when the hook is open end up.)

5. When not using the harness, slide the lines well out of the way, because it is easy to get hooked in inadvertently.

6. Experiment with your line positions to find

the most comfortable. They should be farther forward in lighter air and on reaches. Slide them back as the wind increases or for going upwind.

7. If you get trapped under the sail, underwater and unable to free the line from the hook, use the quick-release buckle to escape from the harness.

SCOOPING AND DEROCKERING
Windsurfer and Windsurfer Rocket boards can be bent by the application of heat and weight followed by cooling. A scoop in the bow alleviates the tendency for the board to pearl (dig under waves) and nose-dive. It also helps you sail over whitewater, rather than trying to punch your way through. For sailing in surf and rough water many people find a 12-inch scoop suitable. For general sailing in chop most people find a 6-inch scoop adequate. Measure scoop by laying the board on the ground and measuring the height of the nose above the ground.

To scoop the bow you'll need a piece of black plastic, such as a garbage bag, and a hot sunny day. (Other sources of heat are boiling water or infrared heat lamps, but be careful not to put lamps too close to the board or you may bubble the plastic and delaminate the deck.)

Tape the plastic to the bottom of the board in front of the mast step and, finding a place in the hot sun and out of the wind, wedge the bows under something convenient like a car bumper, as in figure 10. The fulcrum of the bending process should be located halfway between the mast step and the bow, so put something such as a block of wood under this point. Then put 50 to 70 pounds of weight just behind the daggerboard well. The longer you leave the board in this position the more permanent will be the scoop.

After several hours remove the plastic and cool the board thoroughly with water. Only after it has cooled completely should you remove the weight.

Sailors have found that removing the upward bend of the tail (known as the "rocker") increases the speed of Windsurfers in planing conditions. You can remove the rocker by using the same procedure as for scooping, but with the following changes:

1. Tape the plastic to the deck behind the daggerboard well,

2. Place the fulcrum (for example, a block of

Fig. 10 *Scooping a sailboard*

wood) halfway between the daggerboard well and the stern, and

3. Place the weight just in front of the mast step.

Keep in mind that polyethylene has a memory and will tend to return to its original shape. Thus, in your scooping and derockering efforts you'll have to bend the board two to four times the amount you want to leave in the board.

While on the subject of modifications to Windsurfer hulls, it is worth mentioning that for better traction you can make grooves on the deck with a wood rasp. Apply these grooves at right angles to the directions your feet push.

FREESTYLE

7

SATURDAY AT THE BEACH

Late Saturday morning you come cruisin' out to the beach, your Windsurfer atop your cool green MG. You check out the scene: the sun hot enough to melt the sand, the sand covered with beach towels, beach towels covered with girls, and the girls hot enough to melt the sand. You gaze through your shades at the sun, the girls, the white capping water and say to yourself "Aww-right," cause you're cool, you're the Freestyle Kid.

Casually but carefully, you rig the board, conscious of curious glances straying your way. Now is no time to trip over your mast.

You push the board to the water. Adrenalin starts to pump and your mind clicks into gear with the 15-knot breeze. It's just you and your board on a date with wind and water.

The wind gusts, you hike out and the board accelerates. You tilt the sail, bank the hull and pull "G's" in a 180° jibe. The gut thrill of your maneuver prompts you to head off, pull a flare, splash to a halt, then jibe over. A pirouette, then a duck tack, the fun of learning the tricks overtaken by the sheer pleasure of doing. Move after move brings its own particular high. You are oblivious to the passage of time until finally, spent by your session with wind and water, you return to shore. You land the board, the amateur photographers scatter, and you flop down in the sand to soak up its heat. Rolling onto your back into warmer sand, sighing with satisfaction, you lay an arm across your eyes to shade out the sun. Then a voice disturbs your reverie. "Excuse me, is this a sail surfer?" In the glare of the sun stands someone brown, with long blond hair and a white bikini. You smile, but not too broadly ('cause you're cool), and say to yourself, "Aww-right!"

Freestyle. Just playing around on your board. It's fun, it's absorbing. It's also good exercise. Trying new moves and improving old moves enhance your feel for the wind and your ability to make the board do what you wish. You become a better sailor all around. It's satisfying to discipline and control your body to perform tricks smoothly and artistically. And if others appreciate your accomplishments, that's so much the better.

FROM HOTDOGGING TO FREESTYLE

Hotdogging is what freestyle was originally called. And it's what freestyle was, until recently. Hotdoggers are show-offs who do unusual, spectacular tricks and maneuvers on skis, surfboards, skateboards and suchlike. The name connotes wild lack of discipline, lack of concern for life and skull.

Freestyle, on the other hand, connotes spectacular performances more like those in figure skating and gymnastic floor routines. Technically impeccable displays of athletic skill done in graceful, artistic fashion. It is in this direction that traditional windsurfing freestyle is headed. At the same time there will probably be parallel development of competitive wave/high wind oriented hotdogging. This topic is discussed in chapter 11.

In 1975 when Mike Waltze won the North American Hotdogging Contest, hotdogging was the appropriate name. The routines were undisciplined, the contestants just having a good time, and the judges ad hoc.

In the 1976 Windsurfer North American Championships Dennis Davidson of Hawaii performed a snappy routine to edge out Waltze

---

Freestyle trick such as this pirouette by Ken Winner brings gymnastic skill and grace to windsurfing

for the trophy. Again, it was a casual, careless affair.

Then in 1977 Tropical Blend, the suntan lotion manufacturer, sponsored a windsurfing team to perform freestyle at dozens of North American beaches and lakes. Tropical Blend also sponsored district freestyle champions to the Windsurfer North American Championships, and the North American champion to the Windsurfer World Championships. This commercial sponsorship, and the fact that the event was held at the World Championships, boosted hotdogging to the verge of freestyle respectability. But even that year the routines of the winner* were still clumsy, fraught with errors or falls, and performed in front of judges who were still as mystified as ever about what was going on.

It was in 1978 at the Windsurfer North American Championships, and then at the Windsurfer World Championships in Cancun, Mexico, that freestyle competition reached a maturity worthy of the name. The routine of the competitor who won the North Americans* had, for the first time, no falls or glaring breaks. The routines of the top ten competitors at the World Championships that year showed control, continuity and difficulty seldom before seen—never before seen from so many competitors. Of course, the excellence of the routines at the World Championships left the judges more baffled and divided than ever before. In fact, it left everyone baffled and divided, and with different ideas of who placed where. And it wasn't until the awards banquet four days later that we learned of Matt Schweitzer's triumph in that tough competition.

In 1979 came the introduction of compulsory tricks and a swing in the attitude of judges toward encouraging polished performances. Hence, at the Windsurfer International Regatta held that year at Clearwater Beach, Florida, Gary Eversole of Miami, who received a standing ovation for his excellent control and spectacular tricks, placed third, a victim of too many falls. First place went to a competitor* whose routine lacked radical tricks, but whose execution was judged to be the most polished.

This competition showed a change in the

---

*First place on these occasions went to Ken Winner.

judging system, more experienced, confident judges, and a high level of proficiency by the competitors. Stylish freestyle had finally arrived.

LEARNING TRICKS
Depending upon your approach, learning a new trick can be difficult or relatively easy. A haphazard hit-or-miss (hit or miss the universal with your foot) approach is by far the most common and painful. This usually involves repeated abortive attempts at some move beyond the sailor's ability. Probably most of us have used this approach one time or another, and to be fair, with some success. It's great fun just to go out and play, try new things. In fact, many new tricks are discovered that way. But unfortunately, if you are trying to learn a specific trick, this method can be frustrating and painful. The trick can take longer to learn than necessary, and still be only a clumsy imitation of the real thing. Therefore, in place of a relatively haphazard approach, try a more organized attack.

Identify a trick
Identify the trick you wish to learn. Watch someone else do it, read about it or dream it up on your own. Figure out what actions the trick requires and estimate the forces involved.

Practice on land
You can learn many tricks to a large extent before you even go onto the water. Just find a sandy beach with unobstructed wind, take the skeg off your board and point it in the appropriate direction—for example, into the wind for a duck tack, a close reach for a pirouette. You can get a good feel for most tricks this way.

Ideal water conditions
The first time you practice on water try to find ideal conditions:

Flat water: the smoother the better.

Shallow water: 2 or 3 feet, over a clean sandy bottom, reduces the effort of getting up after a fall.

Steady wind: different strengths for different tricks; 10 knots is good for learning most tricks.

Warmth: anything less than 24°C. (75°F.) is chilly, and constricting wet suits must be worn. If it's too cold you won't want to risk falling in.

Learning procedure

As you progress with a trick, stop frequently and evaluate yourself. Are you progressing, are you rushing things, should you go back a step? Avoid the rut of trying, falling, cursing, trying, falling . . .

For a precise picture of your learning procedure refer to the Freestyle Flow Chart.

Mental technique

To a large extent, what happens in your head is what determines whether you learn a trick well or not. Work on these three concerns: feel, visualization, concentration.

Feel: since you can't stand outside yourself and observe what you're doing, you have to rely upon your other senses to tell you whether you're operating smoothly, in balance and in control. If you don't feel perfectly secure doing a trick then you can do it much better.

Visualize: just before you do a trick try to visualize it. For example, before doing a pirouette get "set": head on a close reach, then tilt and luff the sail just the right amount and imagine your body going through its sequence of motions. Doing the actual pirouette will follow naturally from visualizing it correctly. Visualization probably doesn't work in backgammon but it is indispensable in freestyle.

Concentrate: after the first few years concentration is the single most important factor contributing to good freestyle. It enables you to make good use of limited practice time. A good freestylist will do a trick concentrating on his feet, for example, to ensure they behave correctly; if he discovers a problem he sets it right. Above all, concentrate on doing the trick *correctly*. If you do a trick poorly one hundred times you are learning to do it poorly. It'll take another one hundred good executions to erase the ill effects. Each time you try a duckspin tack and fall you weaken your feel for the duckspin tack and reinforce your feel for the duckspin splash, which rates somewhat lower with the judges.

FREESTYLE FLOW CHART

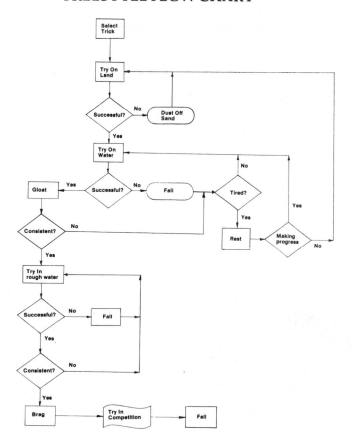

Fig. 1A *Light air head dip*

Fig. 1B

SELECTED TRICKS

There are hundreds of tricks, and new tricks are being developed all the time. We describe a few of special interest. Some are notable for their place in freestyle history, some simply for being especially popular; others are notable for difficulty, and a few for particular elegance and esthetic appeal.

Head dip (fig. 1)

To do this most ancient of tricks you need about 12 knots of wind. Hike out on a close reach with your back arched. Don't try to lean right down to the water at first, but rather lean back several times, each time a little farther. Arch your back, bend your knees and, most importantly, don't stall the sail; that is, concentrate on not sheeting in too much.

Water start (fig. 2)

The water start is one of the more valuable

Fig. 2A *Light air water start*

v

vi

vii

viii

ix

Fig. 1C

Fig. 1D

moves to learn. It can save you the effort of clambering aboard and pulling up the sail after every little fall. In fact, to really learn how, you should try to water start after every fall in more than 12 knots.

First, sail very slowly on a close reach, then luff your sail and fall backward into the water. Refill the sail, bend your knees, and a puff should pull you out of the water. If the wind is light, quickly grab the mast 1 to 2 feet above the deck with

your forward hand. The better leverage of the mast plus the high angle of the sail should produce the necessary force.

If the wind is strong, luff the sail so the board won't rail up while you're in the water, and so you won't be pulled over into the sail after you get up.

Throughout the water start, steer the board in the normal way to keep it perpendicular to the wind. You must also trim the sail so it doesn't stall.

Fig. 2B

Fig. 3 *Sailing back to back*

Back to back (fig. 3)

Back to the leeward side (or back) of the sail was popularized by Dennis Davidson in 1976. Its appeal lies in the fact that instead of hanging onto the booms and struggling madly to maintain balance and grip, as all boardsailors do at some time, the sailor casually leans back against the sail as if it were an easy chair.

To get smoothly into the back-to-back position, sail on a close reach, luff, grasp the mast with your back hand and release with your front hand. Now step around the mast to the leeward side with your back foot, pass the mast to your front hand behind your back, tilt the sail forward, still luffing, and place your back hand on the boom. Lean back to sheet in.

Once you are sailing on the leeward side you'll find you have to be a bit more sensitive to the wind and sail in order to avoid being slammed into the water face first.

Fig. 4A *Duck tack*

Fig. 4B

Fig. 5A *Sail 360*

Fig. 5B

Fig. 5C

Fig. 5D

Fig. 5E

Duck tack (fig. 4)

Though sailors of traditional yachts consider tacking under the sail to be the natural course of things—the way God intended man to tack—for boardsailors it isn't normal and therefore must be considered a freestyle trick.

Head up as in a normal tack until just past head to wind, then tilt the luffing sail forward into the eye of the wind. Slide your forward hand back on the boom as the foot of the sail rises to a height convenient for you to step under.

As you step under, pull the sail back and slightly to the side away from you. Quickly grab the boom on the new tack and bear off.

Be sure to tilt the sail directly into the wind, don't be afraid to let go of the rig entirely, and be quick and sure in your actions.

Sail 360 (fig. 5)

Sometimes called a helicopter, the sail 360 involves turning the sail through 360° by rotating the clew to leeward, over the front of the board, then through the eye of the wind. It is an excellent trick in all conditions, fast and spectacular in heavy air, graceful and artistic in light air.

Try it first in about 5 knots of wind.

Head on a beam reach, luff the sail and tilt the mast to windward (in stronger winds tilt the mast more than in lighter winds). Next, lean into the sail some and rotate it so that it backs. Push with your back hand so that the clew passes over the

Fig. 6A *Clew 360*

Fig. 6B

Fig. 6C

Fig. 6D

bow and through the eye of the wind. After the clew passes through the eye of the wind it will want to finish the 360 very quickly; extend your arms and shuffle or hop quickly into the normal sailing stance.

There are two keys to doing this trick successfully:

1. When you initially luff the sail and tilt the mast to windward, be sure to tilt it far enough.

2. Lean well into the sail initially, so that when it whips around in the second 180° you can extend your arms and squat down to control it.

Clew 360 (fig. 6)

The clew 360 is simply a sail 360 begun from a sailing "clew first" position. Since you don't have to power the clew through the eye of the wind until the end of the 360° turn, by which time you've built up some momentum, it is easier to do this quickly than it is the sail 360.

Starting on a beam reach, sailing with the clew forward, rotate your body and sail 180° with the

clew going initially to leeward. Lean against the pull of the sail until you're on the leeward side, then lean forward against the sail and bend your arms. Continue turning quickly. Force the clew through the eye of the wind by pushing on the back half of the boom, and finish with arms once again extended.

Spin tack (fig. 7)

Fig. 7A *Spin tack*

Fig. 7B

Fig. 7C

Fig. 7D

Fig. 7E

Fig. 7F

Fig. 7G

The spin tack is another of those tricks that are difficult, good-looking, yet possible in almost all conditions.

Start on port tack (for this example), close reaching, with both feet behind the mast. Head up and when headed into the wind release the boom with your right hand as you spin 180° clockwise on your left foot. Place your right foot in front of the mast step, release the boom with your left hand, grab the mast with your right hand and continue your spin on the ball of your right foot. As you complete your spin, tilt the sail forward, grab the boom with your left hand, grab the boom with your right hand, and sheet in. Precise timing and rhythm are necessary for smooth execution.

Fig. 8A

Fig. 8B *Duckspin tack*

Fig. 8C

Fig. 8D

Fig. 9A

Fig. 9B   *Pirouette*

Fig. 9C

Fig. 9D

Fig. 10A *Flare*

Duckspin tack (fig. 8)

After the duck tack and the spin tack, the next logical step in fancy tricks is the duckspin tack. Jim Kortright of Sarasota, Florida developed this trick and does it in a unique way; he tilts the sail forward so that it is perfectly balanced and motionless, squats down, spins, then straightens up and sails away on the new tack. Most people, however, do it an easier way:

Head up on starboard tack (for this example) and slide your right hand back on the booms as you tilt the sail forward into the wind. As the foot of the sail reaches head height, place your left foot in front of your right. Then, as you duck under and initiate a 360° clockwise spin on your right foot, pull the sail back a little and slightly to starboard. Sail away on port tack.

Matt Schweitzer uses a method in which he reaches from one boom to the other while his back is to the sail. Different methods have their own strong points, but Jim's probably looks best.

Pirouette (fig. 9)

The pirouette is one of the more elegant and versatile tricks. Once you've learned it, you can do it in heavy or light air, calm or rough water.

Close reach on port tack (for this example), luff the sail slightly and tilt it to weather. It is important that you place your sail carefully and let go of it cleanly so that it will be where you can reach it when you complete your pirouette. Spin clockwise on the outside ball of your right foot, tuck your hands and arms close to your chest, keep your back straight, and kick out with your left foot as you complete your spin. Kicking out with your foot slows your turn and allows you a little more time to spot the boom and grab it. Don't rush your pirouette.

A double pirouette—a continuous 720° spin on one foot only—is many times more difficult, but similar in execution to the single.

Warning: the writers have determined that this trick can rub the skin off your foot.

Fig. 10B

Flare (fig. 10)

The flare—or wheelie, as it's also known—is no more than a tail sink in light air, but looks spectacular in strong winds.

You'll need a high-wind daggerboard if it's windy enough to bother doing this trick. Head off to a broad reach, squat halfway down, then spring to the stern of the board and pull up on the booms. You must land squarely on the stern; too much weight to the right side and you'll turn left, and vice versa. If you have enough wind and are going very fast, the board will skip along on its tail, nose pointing skyward.

Fig. 11A *Railride*

Fig. 11B

Fig. 11C

Fig. 11D

Fig. 11E

Railride (fig. 11)
After Robby Naish introduced it to a wider public at the 1976 Windsurfer World Championships, the railride caught on and became *the* thing to do, although Matt Schweitzer and Mike Waltze had, in fact, been doing a slightly different railride for several years.

Try it first while sailing on a close or beam reach on smooth water, in 10 or 12 knots of wind.

Step to leeward slightly with your back foot and put your weight on the booms and on your back leg. Now squat down and slip your forward foot under the windward rail, and flip the board on its side. Your weight will transfer to your forward shin (Owww!) as you lift your back foot onto the rail. Pull down to the booms to lift your forward foot onto the rail.

It helps to have your mast foot stuck tightly in the board so that you can lean the windward rail against the mast. But don't lean the rail too hard or you'll risk breaking your mast or delaminating your deck.

Should the mast foot come out of the board you may fall on your daggerboard and break it— break it or puncture a kidney (fun, isn't it?)—so use an old, blunt daggerboard.

Flare jibe (fig. 12)
An excellent jibe for freestyle, the flare jibe was

Fig. 12A *Flare jibe*

Fig. 12B

Fig. 12C

Fig. 12D

first used extensively in competition by Mark Robinson.

Head off, do a flare, but when you spring back put more weight on the windward side of the board and tilt your sail slightly to that side, as well. The board will spin 90° or more on its tail. Step quickly forward to stop the spin and then swing your sail around to the new tack. Remember to step forward smartly or the board will continue to turn right into the wind.

Everoll (fig. 13)
Introduced by Gary Eversole of Florida in 1979, the Everoll—sailing the board upside down—further separates racers and freestylists. For while racers have always prized grapeskin-smooth undersides for fast sailing, freestylists are now taking rasps to the planing surface of their boards, to improve their footing.

Try the trick in 8 to 10 knots. Sail on a beam reach, clew first, and flip the board on the rail as you would for a regular railride. This time, however, the board will lean to leeward so much

that you'll be able to put your feet on the underside.

Control of board angle is opposite to that for the railride. To tilt the board more to windward don't sheet out, sheet in. To tilt to leeward more and get it more upside down, sheet out.

Note: to perform this trick successfully you must fix your universal *very* firmly into your board.

Fig. 13 *Everoll*

Back flip (fig. 14)
In the back flip, another spectacular trick developed by Gary Eversole, the body passes feet first between the windward boom and the sail.

Try it first in about 12 to 15 knots of wind and only with a very heavily reinforced mast and strong aluminum booms. Sail on a close reach,

Fig. 14   *Back flip*

luff a bit, then kick up and through the booms with your feet. Don't be tentative. You have to kick up strongly and then bend your knees so that you are in a semi-tuck position. As long as you kick up hard, and tuck so that you complete the flip quickly, you have a good chance of landing on the board.

The splits
This is an elegant trick, particularly when executed by women's freestyle champion Rhonda Smith of Miami, Florida. Rhonda describes her approach to the trick:

"The thing about this trick is that you have to know how to do the splits before you get on a sailboard, but then you can do it in any kind of wind. I start on starboard tack on a close reach. I start sliding my front foot forward and as it gets about 3 feet forward I start sliding my back foot back till I'm down, my front foot pointing forward, my back leg at a 45° angle with the front leg.

"If your booms are high, drop your front hand to hold your mast, and hold your booms with your back hand. You tend to head up a bit. If there's a lot of wind you tend to head up quite a lot and then there's a little bit of strength necessary. In light wind it takes no strength at all.

"To get back up, if there's wind you just bring both feet in real quick and you end up in a sitting position, and then you stand up. If the wind is light you have to be very careful not to fall when getting up.

"The difference in doing the splits in high wind is that I can go down and touch and come right back up within a couple of seconds. In over 20-knots wind I may head up quickly, so I have to do the splits and recover really quickly."

Splits and head dip combination
Rhonda is also known for a splits and head dip combination. For this trick you need fairly strong wind to hold you up since, as Rhonda says, "it isn't like a head dip where you can always move your body inward to stop falling, because you're spread out on the board.

"To do the head dip from a splits position, arch your back considerably. I hold the mast with my forward hand quite a way below the booms but above my head so I can control heading up. Watch your sail to avoid heading up. As soon as your sail starts to luff just the smallest bit, throw your back hand forward and your front hand forward and bear off. But don't bear off so much that you have too much sail area to handle. It's good to have a little bit of luff if there's a lot of wind."

DEVELOPING A ROUTINE
Why a routine?
If you think having a routine is stultifying and that freestyle should be free and spontaneous, remember that the objective is to appear free and spontaneous, not necessarily to be free and spontaneous. The finest examples of music and art are painstakingly planned and carefully executed. The same applies to windsurfing freestyle. A planned routine serves to aid your memory so that you do all your tricks and don't end up standing out there on the water trying to think of something to do. It also helps you fit more moves into a given period of time, and permits you to choreograph your moves so they

flow smoothly from one to the next. At first you won't be smooth. You'll feel hurried and awkward doing tricks in quick succession. But with practice they'll meld together as if there was no other way to do them.

Put it on paper
Start your work by listing all the tricks you can do nine times out of ten. These are the tricks to put in your routine at first. What good is a routine if you have to climb out of the water between tricks?

Now arrange the tricks in a sequence. Your tricks may suggest their own natural order, for elegance, flow, etc. Once you have a routine, go out and try it. It can probably be improved, so think about it, then make changes. Add tougher tricks after you master them.

Play to your audience
Design the routine to keep you in center stage, near the judges. It's no good wandering off in your own little world where no one can see what you're doing. Also, if possible, stay to leeward of

1. Water start
2. Railride
3. Backward railride
4. Duck Tack
5. Flare Jibe

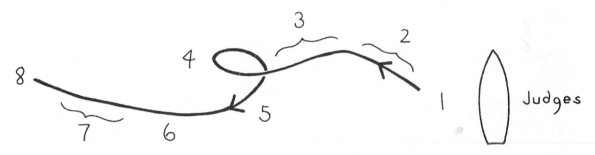

6. Sail 360
7. Leeward Railride
8. Pirouette

Fig. 15   *Badly grouped combination of tricks*

1. Water Start
2. Railride
3. Duck Tack
4. Sail 360
5. Pirouette
6. Backward Railride
7. Flare Jibe
8. Leeward Railride

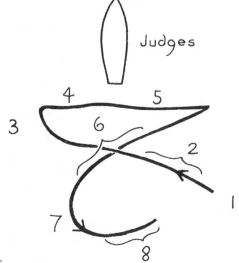

Fig. 16   *Effectively grouped combination of tricks*

the judges so that they can see you instead of just the sail.

It helps to draw your routine on paper so you can juggle the order to fulfill the objectives. Figure 15 shows poor order. The freestylist is wandering across the water. Figure 16 shows the same tricks rearranged to keep the sailor in one area.

Use combinations

Combinations done well make your routine richer with tricks, imparting a sense of continuity and wholeness, so that a collection of dissimilar actions is transformed into an artistic whole.

Sequences of related tricks are especially effective. For example, design a combination of four moves in which the sail turns 180° in the course of each move. These should be distinct tricks, yet related, and at no time during the sequence is the sailor in a normal position. Grouping related tricks together also uses the time more efficiently. For example, do several tricks on a forward railride, then when you get off the rail don't do another forward railride. A good example of a combination is one Cort Larned of Miami used in 1978 at the North American and World Windsurfer Championships:

1. Sailing back to sail on leeward side
to
2. Tack
to
3. Back to sail on windward side
to
4. Nose dip

These four distinct tricks are melded into one with a minimum of wasted time and motion.

Be original

Keep in mind that judges see the same tricks, even the same combinations of tricks, many times. Therefore you'll find them very appreciative of anything different. So keep an eye on what your competition is doing, and do a few things differently. Or if one person is doing something that's different and good, copy him. Don't strive to be superbrilliantly imaginative. Just vary your routines enough to keep out of a rut and maintain fresh perspective.

Originality can easily be carried past the point of usefulness, though. In Cancun, at the 1978 World Championships, there was a finalist who turned his board upside down, stuck his "T" in the daggerboard well and sailed away. Different, certainly. But difficult, graceful, artistic? Decidedly not.

Refine your performance

Good execution makes your routine stand out. No matter how good the continuity and originality of your routine, or the difficulty of your tricks, poor execution will ruin you. Mark Robinson is known for his snappy, powerful, stylish execution, a trait that has carried him to the top rank of freestylists.

To achieve good execution you need to be dissatisfied with just doing a trick. You must want to dance a trick. Don't be satisfied with struggling through a spin tack in four clumsy steps, for example, but strive to do it in two steps, with perfect balance and no hesitation.

To improve execution keep these things in mind:

1. Be quick but not hasty.
2. Make no unnecessary motions. Actions should be smooth, continuous and direct.
3. Once you've mastered a trick, think about adding motions for stylistic flair—for example, perhaps an arm extended skyward during a pirouette would serve this purpose.

As judges become more sophisticated they will become increasingly aware of the fine points of freestyle routines. In the future, attention to these details will make the difference between first and last place in competition.

MAINTENANCE

8

Now that you've done a little freestyle you can probably recognize the need for a chapter on maintenance. After wavesailing, freestyle abuses your board more than any other kind of sailing. The following are a few problem areas which you should be competent to correct.

FIBERGLASS HULL REPAIR

Fiberglass hulls are fairly light and strong, but are easily damaged. Serious damage should be repaired by a professional, if you want a good job. But you can fix small dents or cracks yourself. You'll need:

- Electric drill to adapt to 50-grit sanding disk.
- 4-ounce fiberglass cloth.
- Polyester sanding resin (make sure you get sanding resin, as other types stay gummy even after setting up).
- Hardener.
- Acetone.
- Three or four throwaway paintbrushes.
- Surgical gloves.
- Scissors.
- Plastic mixing cup.

A dent in a fiberglass board must be repaired before the board is used again, or water will seep in and cause the glass to delaminate from the foam.

With the drill and sanding disk and some 50-grit sandpaper, grind away the damaged fiberglass so that the area has a very shallow dish-shaped hollow. Grind just through to the foam.

Cut several pieces of fiberglass to the shape and size of the dish, and clean the area with acetone.

Mix a small quantity of resin, according to the directions on the container.

Paint a coat of resin onto the dished area. Paint a piece of fiberglass, using enough resin to saturate it, then brush out excess resin. Lay the saturated fiberglass onto the dished area. Paint another piece of fiberglass and brush out excess resin, as for the first piece, and lay this piece on top of the first. Continue to add glass, making sure to saturate each piece thoroughly without, however, using more resin than necessary. Allow to set for the length of time specified on the container, then grind down the repaired area so it is smooth and level with the surrounding hull. Add another coat of resin.

POLYETHYLENE HULL REPAIR

Polyethylene hulls have the advantage of not damaging easily, but the disadvantage of not repairing easily. The most common trouble area is the daggerboard well. Cracks and cuts tend to appear in the aft end of the well (particularly with older Windsurfers, those without aluminum "tacos" in the well) as a result of running aground, or even just pulling the daggerboard out too roughly. You may also have problems with voids or soft spots in the foam.

To make repairs you'll need:
- Knife.
- Wire coat hanger.
- Epoxy resin and solvent.
- Paper towels.
- Large plastic syringe.
- Electric drill and 3/8-inch bit.

Enlarge the crack in the daggerboard well with a knife, so that you can break up and scrape out the foam behind with the coat hanger. Next, dry the foam by letting the board sit in a warm, dry place all winter, or with a hair dryer, or by poking the corner of a paper towel into the foam and drawing the water out by capillary action.

Once the foam is dry, stand the board on its stern (if the crack is in the back of the well), mix a slow-setting epoxy and pour it into the crack. The epoxy should be a slow-setting type or it will generate a lot of heat, "boil" up out of the crack and make a mess. Allow the epoxy to set for twenty-four hours before using the board.

If you need to fill a void such as around a wobbly mast step or under a footstrap, it is better to use epoxy than foam. If foam failed once it'll probably fail again; epoxy has much greater compressive strength. Furthermore, foam expands so much when it goes off that you'll run the risk of causing damage with it.

Drill two $\frac{3}{8}$-inch holes into the void or soft foam area, but make them as far apart as possible. Break up the bad foam inside with the coat hanger, and make sure there is a passage from one hole to the other.

Mix the epoxy, pour it into the syringe, and place the nozzle of the syringe into the lower of the two holes. Squirt epoxy into the void until it starts coming out of the upper hole. Continue adding epoxy until the void has been entirely filled. If the epoxy goes off hot it'll bubble up through the holes, but in this case there's no need for concern because you can grind off the excess after it has set.

MASTS

If you plan to use your masts roughly, reinforce them in three key places—the butt, the tip, and the area where the booms attach. You'll need:

- 8-ounce fiberglass tape (like cloth but in narrow strips), 6 inches wide and 12 inches wide.
- Sandpaper, 50 grit.
- Epoxy resin (polyester will not work).
- Acetone and rag.
- Plastic milk jug.
- Scissors.
- Hacksaw.
- Thin plastic surgical-type gloves.

Prepare the surfaces to be reinforced by sanding with coarse-grit sandpaper and then cleaning with a rag soaked in acetone. Put on gloves, then mix a few ounces of epoxy resin in the cutoff bottom of the milk jug, and saturate the fiberglass tape by dipping it in the resin. Use as little resin as possible, while still saturating the fiberglass. Wrap the tape onto the prepared area (fig. 1) and leave to harden.

This method of reinforcing keeps the booms from crushing the mast, keeps the base and tip of the mast from splitting, and yet doesn't seriously affect the overall flexibility.

To fix a broken mast, use a section from another broken mast to serve as an outside sleeve or internal pin. You can usually arrange the three pieces as in figure 2, though the type of repair depends upon the extent of the damage.

With a strong pin fixed to the inside of the repair area with epoxy resin, you can then wrap fiberglass on the outside as you did to reinforce the mast.

To repair a split butt-end of a mast, simply bind the broken area into its original sound shape with

Glass must be thickest at mast base so 2 wraps are used.

First: 3 wraps of 12-inch-wide fiberglass

Second: 3 wraps of 6-inch-wide fiberglass

Where booms attach: 5 wraps of 12-

Mast tip: 3 wraps of 6-inch fiberglass

Fig. 1 *Masts should be reinforced with fiberglass*

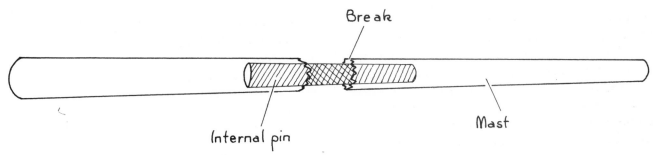

Fig. 2   *Mend a broken mast with an internal pin*

heavy synthetic thread (fig. 3) and then fiberglass as described for reinforcement. If the broken butt has already been reinforced, grind off all the reinforcing material before reglassing.

BOOMS

Most booms are made of bent aluminum tubes joined at the ends by injection-molded plastic, usually nylon. Foam plugs seal the ends of the tubing, rivets secure the plastic boom ends to the tubing, and synthetic rubber covers the aluminum. Should the rubber tear badly, the tubes kink, the ends break or the plugs leak, you'll need to separate the ends from the tubes.

For the following repairs you'll need:
- $3/16$-inch by $1/2$-inch stainless steel pop rivets and a pop rivet gun.
- Electric drill and $3/16$-inch bit.
- Two bicycle innertubes, approximately $1\frac{3}{8}$-inch in diameter.
- Bicycle pump (preferably a foot pump, to leave your hands free).
- Neoprene cement.
- Acetone.
- Sandpaper, 50 grit.
- Throwaway paintbrush.
- Scissors.
- Silicone-base caulking.
- Duct tape.
- Vise grips or C-clamp.
- Styrofoam.

To replace an end or tube, simply drill out the rivets with a $3/16$-inch bit. Replace the broken parts, drill any necessary holes, then rivet the ends back on.

To plug the end of a tube, apply a generous bead of silicone caulking around the inside. Then, using the tube as a cookie cutter, stamp out a plug from a piece of Styrofoam and shove it a couple of inches into the tube. The caulking should prevent water leaking past the plug.

Should the grip on your booms be poor, or the covering be coming off, you can apply your own covering made from a bicycle innertube. This will be better than many stock coverings. Bicycle innertube, once roughened, has excellent grip and will last a season or two.

The instructions below describe a technique for putting an innertube on in one piece, tightly, so that it really stays on.

1. First, sand the aluminum tube with coarse sandpaper in the area to be covered, then clean both tube and innertube with a rag soaked in acetone.

2. Cut the innertube 2 inches from the valve stem and seal the end nearest the stem by clamping it with two slats of wood put between the jaws of a vise grip or C-clamp (fig. 6).

3. Start the other end of the innertube onto a wood mast tip, turning the first inch of innertube inside itself to form a lip as illustrated in figure 4. (This 1-inch lip forms an airtight seal and allows

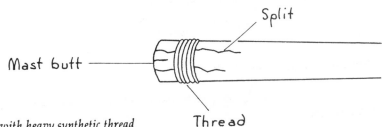

Fig. 3   *Bind a split mast end with heavy synthetic thread*

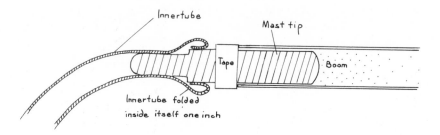

Innertube

Mast tip

Tape

Boom

Innertube folded inside itself one inch

Fig. 4

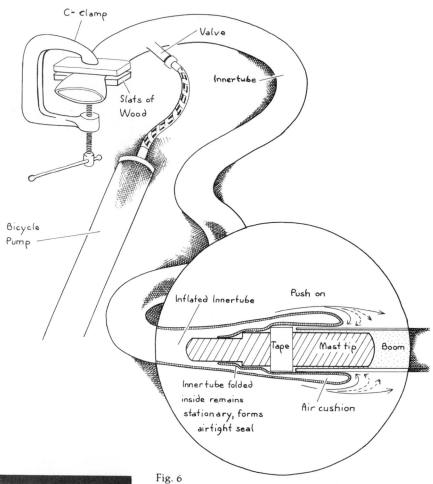

C-clamp

Valve

Innertube

Slats of Wood

Bicycle Pump

Inflated Innertube

Push on

Tape   Mast tip   Boom

Innertube folded inside remains stationary, forms airtight seal

Air cushion

Fig. 6

Partially inflate innertube and push onto boom

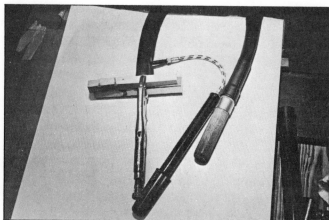

Fig. 5 *Setup for covering boom*

the inflated innertube to slide over the seal, onto the aluminum.) Wrap tape around the mast tip so it can only go into the boom about 3 inches, and insert the mast tip into the end of the boom. Secure the other end of the boom in a vise, to allow you both hands free to pull the innertube on.

4. Apply a coat of neoprene cement to the prepared aluminum, let it set for 10 minutes, then apply another coat.

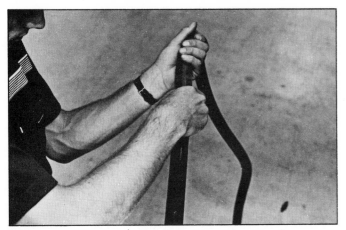
Fig. 7A
End of boom should be in vise to leave both hands free to push on innertube

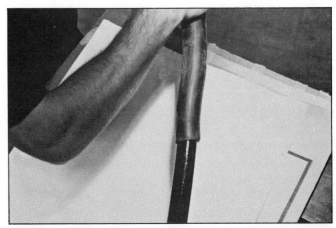
Fig. 7B

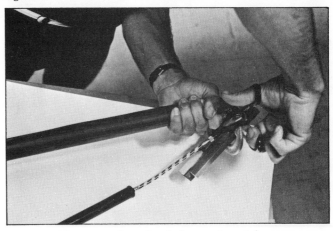
Fig. 8 *Hold air in with one hand, then cut innertube*

5. Immediately, inflate the innertube with the bicycle pump, till the tube is a bit larger in diameter than the aluminum. Remove the pump and start sliding the innertube over itself, turning it inside out onto the boom. (The innertube goes on much the way you peel a wet suit off.)

6. When the innertube is halfway on, the valve will stop it going any farther. Therefore cut the innertube between the end of the boom and the valve stem, and at the same time prevent the air escaping by clamping your hand around the innertube right at the end of the boom (fig. 8).

7. Now, keeping the air in with your hand around the innertube and boom, quickly continue to slide the innertube over itself onto the boom (fig. 9).

8. Trim the rubber to the correct length, and clean off excess neoprene cement with strong

solvent such as toluene or acetone. Roughen the rubber by rubbing with similar strong solvent or by sandpapering lightly, or leaving to weather in the sun awhile.

This is yet another breakthrough that Windsurfing Hawaii gets credit for.

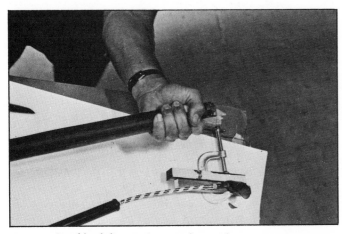
Fig. 9A *Quickly slide rest of innertube over boom*

Fig. 9B

Fig. 10A *Fold from top to bottom*

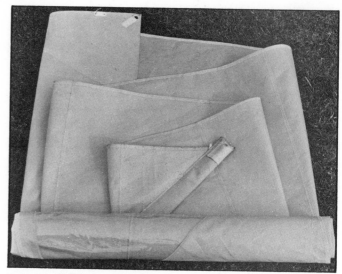

Fig. 10B *Roll from mast tube*

Fig. 11 *Alternately, roll onto mast*

SAILS

The sail is the most delicate part of your sailboard and, for racing, the most important part. If you plan to race in big events such as your National Championships use a fairly new, well-maintained sail. If you've used your racing sail more than a dozen times in over 12 knots, it has probably lost its racing edge. For everyday racing use an old racing sail; for everyday play use a 3.8- to 4.2-ounce battenless sail.

Always remove battens and fold or roll your sails neatly. Figures 10 and 11 show two good ways of storing a sail. In general, rolling is best for the sail, but whichever way you store it, avoid folding it on the windows. (For short periods you can also store the sail with the booms on the mast, by rolling the sail, starting from the clew, so you end up with the rolled sail lying alongside the mast.)

Any tears in the sail should be repaired immediately, before further use distorts the cloth around the tear. And if you want to give your sail the best treatment available, rinse it in fresh water after use in salt water. If it is dirty you can wash it by hand with a mild household detergent, but don't use strong (industrial) detergent, or put the sail in a washing machine, because you'll damage it. Don't put it in a hot-air dryer, either—you'll end up with a Dacron hula-hoop.

UNIVERSALS

Of the two main types of universal joint, the stainless steel type is the strongest and most reliable, but the rubber ones are lighter in weight and not so painful to kick.

Unfortunately, some rubber universals break rather readily and so should not be used in situations where you may have to paddle a long way. Keep an eye on them and if a crack appears in the rubber renew it before it breaks.

The old Windsurfer universals, those with the wooden mast base, tend to break when the mast base gets stuck in the mast and can't rotate. The new ones, patterned after the almost unbreakable universals used originally in Hawaii, are very reliable. They may need a new upper washer (the one at the bottom of the mast base) occasionally, and you should see that the upper swivel bolt is not working its way out of the base; if it is, a few turns with a wrench will snug it up.

DAGGERBOARDS
If you don't have the type of daggerboard that automatically swings back on running aground, it's a useful idea to remove the cap and reshape the part that goes into the daggerboard well (fig. 12) so that it will roll out, under the board, when you hit bottom. Of course, your daggerboard must fit snugly in the well or you'll lose it, so you may need to tape it with the same type of tape used for mast bases (chapt. 2).

Damage to Windsurfers' plastic daggerboards can be repaired with polyester putty, as used for auto-body or boat repair. For small scratches use surfacing putty. For gouges and small chips use Bondo, or similar auto-body filler. Cracks should be enlarged and mended by pouring in epoxy putty.

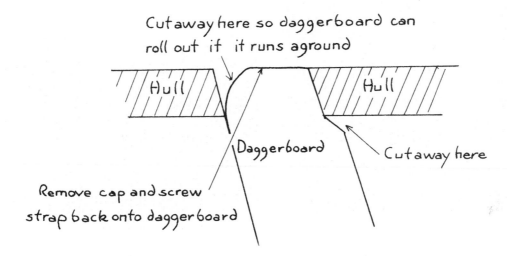

Fig. 12   *Modify your daggerboard so that it swings back on running aground*

RACING—THE BASICS

9

Racing is whatever you want it to be. It can be serious competition, a relaxing day in the sun, or just something you help organize and run for fun and good company. If you are new to racing and want to learn more about it, this chapter should get you on the right tack.

THE COURSE

One of the most widely used racing courses in yacht racing (yes, a sailboard is a yacht) is the Olympic course in figure 1. This puts great emphasis on upwind sailing. A popular variation of this uses the same line for both start and finish, and places this line between marks 1 and 3.

RULES

Most races are sailed under the International Yacht Racing Union (IYRU) rules. One of the first things you should do before playing this game is read these rules. To understand them thoroughly takes intense study, but as long as you understand those numbered 36 to 40 you'll be better off than most novices.

At most sailboard regattas the "720 rule" is in effect. That is, if you foul somebody (run into them when they have right-of-way) you can exonerate yourself by turning your board in two complete consecutive circles—a 720° turn. If the 720 rule is not in effect, the rules state that you should retire from the race upon committing a foul.

SKIPPERS' MEETING

Every race or series of races should be preceded by a skippers' meeting. The purpose of this meeting is to review sailing instructions, answer queries and deal with amendments. Don't miss

this meeting, do pay close attention and do get out to the starting line well before the start. Remember, the race committee may start without you—their job is to start on time.

STARTING

The start is the single most important part of the race, particularly if the race is to be a short one. If you are behind at the start you not only have distance to make up on the leaders, you also have to cope with "dirty air." Dirty air is wind that has been disturbed by the passage of other sails ahead or upwind of you. Hence you should learn how to start at the gun, on the line, and in clear air.

The line

The starting line is the line of sight between two starting marks or boats, as shown in the course diagram (fig. 1). If you are on the wrong side of the line, or if your bow is only two inches over the line when the gun sounds, the race committee spotters will call your number. If you don't go back and restart you'll be disqualified from the race.

Starting sequence

Preceding the starting signal is the starting sequence, a series of flag raisings, gun soundings, whistle blowings or horn honkings which indicate how much time is left before the start. You will have been told the starting sequence at the skippers' meeting. A racing stopwatch will also help you keep track of the time remaining, especially one that counts down rather than up.

Favored end

Five or ten minutes before the start determine

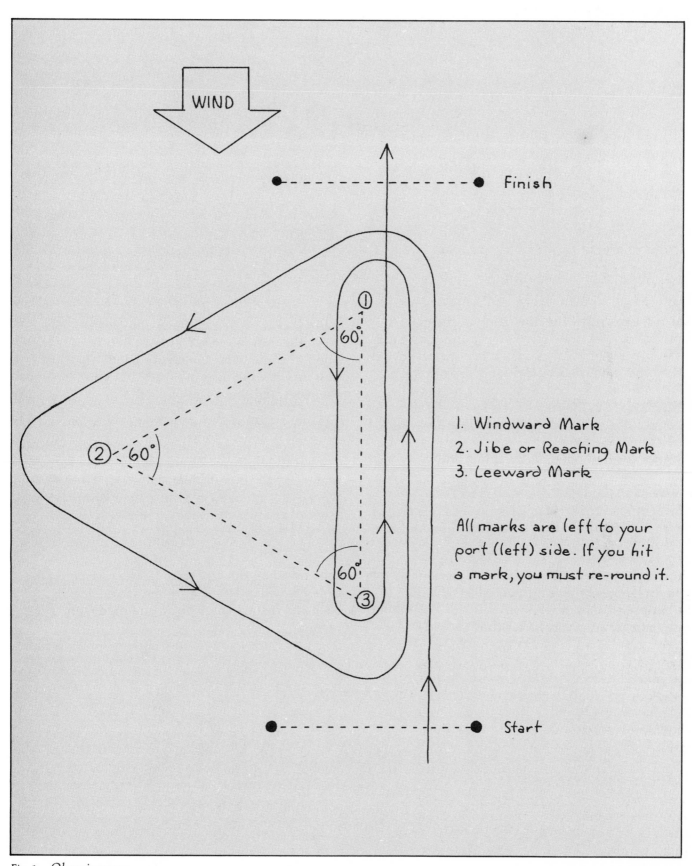

WIND

Finish

① 60°

② 60°

60°

③

1. Windward Mark
2. Jibe or Reaching Mark
3. Leeward Mark

All marks are left to your port (left) side. If you hit a mark, you must re-round it.

Start

Fig. 1 *Olympic course*

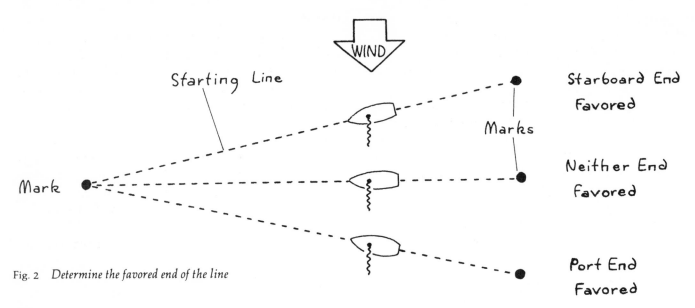

Fig. 2 *Determine the favored end of the line*

the favored end of the line—that is, the most upwind end. Figure 2 shows the procedure. Luff near one end of the line and aim your bow at the other end. If your sail is perpendicular to the centerline of your board, neither end is favored. Otherwise, whichever end the front of your booms point more nearly toward is the favored end.

Since the favored end is upwind, and that's the direction you want to go, starting there puts you ahead of anybody who doesn't start there. Unfortunately, everybody else knows this too, so there is invariably a big crowd at the favored end.

Until you know what you are doing, stay away from the crowd and start about a third of the way down the line from the favored end. This way you may not get the best start, but you won't get the worst, either.

The actual start

As for the actual start, just make sure you are in or near the first row of boards at thirty seconds to go. Use the boards near you as an indication of where the line is. Keep your bow even with the bows of the boards nearby, then with two or three seconds to go, sheet in.

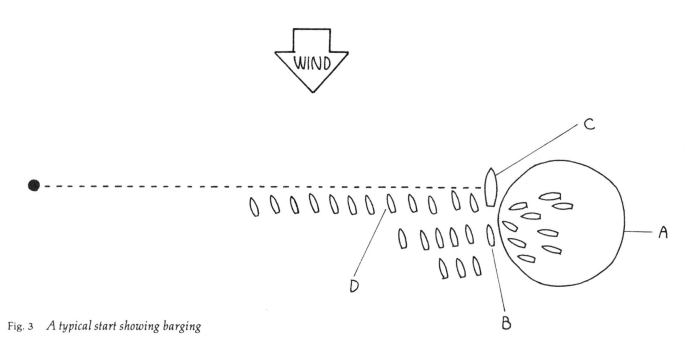

Fig. 3 *A typical start showing barging*

Barging (fig. 3)

All the boats in circle A will try to squeeze between boat B and the starting boat C. Boat B is not obliged to let any of them in, and any boat that tries to squeeze in regardless is "barging." Barging is illegal and should not be tolerated. However, it does have one redeeming characteristic. All those bargers, of whom only one or two will get a good start, leave the rest of the line less cluttered for intelligent starters such as D.

BEATING UPWIND

Once clear of the starting line, your next objective is to get to the windward mark quickly.

Speed

You should point as high into the wind as you can without slipping sideways too much. A good feel for how high you can point comes with experience. Anytime you feel yourself slipping sideways, foot off. That is, bear off a little for more speed.

Wind shifts

As you sail to weather notice how the wind shifts. Every few minutes the wind changes direction slightly. Figure 4 shows how boat A uses these shifts to go to weather more quickly than boat B.

Each dash in the course of each boat represents

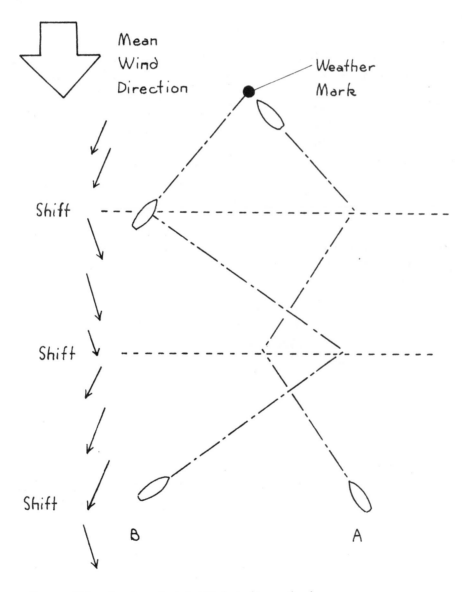

Fig. 4   *Take advantage of wind shifts by tacking on headers*

a unit of distance covered. By the time A reaches the weather mark, B is only three-quarters of the way there. A tacked on the headers. B did the opposite, and ended up pointing lower than A on each tack. You know you've run into a header when you can't point as high as you were, and unless you can see the mark ahead or have a compass, the way to tell you aren't pointing as high is to judge your position relative to other boats. A lift, on the other hand, allows you to point even higher. A good, simple, general rule for making use of windshifts is, "Tack on being headed." That is, every time the wind shifts so as to make you head off a little, tack.

REACHING AND RUNNING

The "free" legs of the course are easier than the beats—that is, unless you fall a lot. Time and again you hear the stories of people who were doing great upwind, but who couldn't stay on their feet on the reaches or on the run.

It helps to pull your daggerboard out during off the wind legs, and on runs you should stand far enough back to keep the bow from pearling (digging into waves).

However, if you're not having problems with balance, your main concern should be keeping clean air. At the start of a reach head high if someone is close behind you so he doesn't try to block your wind and then pass. And when running, especially in light air, get off to the side so that the clump of sails behind you doesn't block your wind.

FINISHING

The finish line has a favored end just as the starting line has, but in this case it is the downwind end. Always try to cross the finish line on the tack most nearly perpendicular to the line,

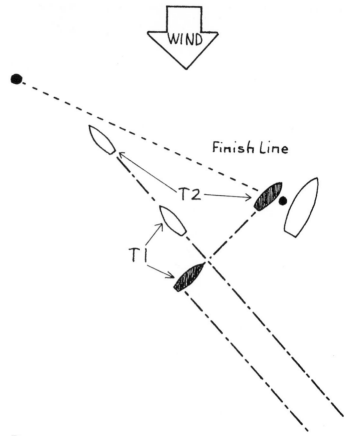

Fig. 5

At time T_1 the white boat was ahead. At this time the black boat tacked, and at time T_2 crossed the favored end of the line to win

and with the mark just to leeward of you (fig. 5).

If neither end of the finishing line is favored, try to make your final tack starboard so that you will have right-of-way in any last-minute encounter.

As mentioned before, this chapter is for the sailor completely new to racing. For a more thorough discussion of aspects of racing unique to sailboards, read the next chapter.

RACING—ADVANCED

10

Racing a sailboard is much like racing any other small sailboat. Rules, tactics, strategy, these things are much the same. However, it does require different techniques to make different boats go fast, and so this chapter discusses "go-fast" techniques unique to sailboard racing, those not found in more general racing books.

EQUIPMENT

In one-design class racing* your equipment is an important part of your race-winning effort. Good equipment promotes good speed and contributes to a winning frame of mind. However, no amount of tinkering and fussing will be as worthwhile as actually getting out on the course and racing. So make any necessary and legal changes (depending on your class rules), then go out and sail.

Rig

Your **sail** is the most delicate and, for racing, the most important part of your boat. Boardsails may have wrinkles from the luff to the clew if the mast tubes are poorly sewn. See that you don't buy a sail that's worse in this respect than the ones your friends are using.

Your **booms** should have an outhaul cleat on each side, if such an arrangement is legal. Metal cleats are best, because pre-stretched line wears out plastic cleats in a few weeks of use.

Lines (inhaul, downhaul, outhaul, vang) should be ¼-inch or ³⁄₁₆-inch pre-stretched, braided Marlow. A bungeed uphaul is easiest to use (see chapter 6).

_____
*Open and development class racing is beyond the scope of this book.

Mast and **universal** shouldn't need any changes. The universal, however, should be stuck firmly (firmly, not utterly immovably) in the mast step of the hull.

Hull

Hulls that can be scooped or de-rockered (chapter 6) should be kept fairly flat for racing. More than 6 inches of bow scoop and more than 2 inches of tail rocker are sure to slow you down in most conditions.

If your hull has scratches on the underside you should sand them smooth. Progress gradually from fine (120 grit) to very fine (600 grit) "wet and dry" sandpaper. Then polish for the fastest finish.

If your polyethylene board has deep gouges you'll have to sand them out. But with a glass board you can fill them with a marine-grade surfacing putty and then sand smooth.

Your **daggerboard** should fit snugly in the well. It should also be perpendicular to the bottom of the hull and parallel with the hull's longitudinal axis. The popular material to use for shimming the daggerboard into a good fit is "duct tape" (see chapter 2).

The **skeg** should be left full size since in most conditions you need maximum directional stability. It should also line up with the daggerboard and be perpendicular to the bottom of the hull.

BOAT SPEED

Boat speed is a good thing to have because being faster than everyone else is like starting a game of Monopoly with the deeds to Boardwalk and Park Place; it makes problems of starting, strategy and tactics just that much easier to handle. So, anything you can legally do to increase your speed is worth the effort.

Sail adjustment

Proper adjustment of a boardsail is not widely different from that of other types of sail. However there are a few exceptions of which to be aware.

Since the booms are located a third of the way up the luff of the sail, tightening the outhaul not only flattens the sail but tightens the leech as well. Hence flattening the sail of a board by ½ inch has a more profound effect than would flattening a more conventional sail by the same amount.

In very light air, less than 2 knots, it pays to flatten your sail, not only because it'll probably have fewer wrinkles but also because every tiny motion of the sail is more effective in propelling the board (if these motions are noticeable, the process is called pumping).

In 15 knots of wind and more your sail should probably be pulled as flat as possible. It depends, of course, on the amount of chop, the cut of the sail and the mast stiffness. But as a general rule it should be flat.

If in heavy air, force 5 or 6, you are having trouble getting through the course, you might try making your sail very full rather than flat. A flat sail is difficult to luff only partly; it tends to be either full or all luffing and thus harder to control. With more belly in it you'll be able to luff just 40 or 50% of the sail with greater ease.

Hull trim

Most of the time, keep your hull flat on the water to promote planing. In particular, tilting the windward rail down is almost always bad.

In light air you can tilt the hull a bit to leeward, to reduce wetted surface and increase lateral resistance upwind. And when you are not planing keep the transom out of the water.

Going upwind in chop you may need to stand aft a bit to let the bow rise more easily to waves. Running in chop you should be just far enough back to keep the bow from burying—but no

Fig. 1 *The "kangaroo grip" is an effective stance when wind is under 12 knots*

farther. (This requires considerable fore and aft shifting of weight).

But as a general rule—keep it flat.

Stance
The "kangaroo grip" is a very effective way to sail in less than 12 knots. Feet and hands are placed close together, arms bent, legs bent at the knees and hips, back straight. Keeping your feet close together takes weight off the ends of the hull so that they lift more readily to the waves. It also forces you to be more in balance at all times.

With your hands close together you are more sensitive to the balance of the sail, which permits you to sense and correct a stall or luff more quickly. Bent arms and knees permit you to adjust for balance and sail trim with minimum disturbance of driving forces.

In very light air, allow the sail to tilt to leeward a bit. Gravity will then help give the sail shape.

As the wind passes 12 knots, adopt more of a straight-arm, spread-foot stance. Keep your hands fairly close together so as to distribute the load evenly between them. However, feet should be spread apart somewhat so that you can steer through waves and handle gusts effectively.

Daggerboard
Whether or not to pull out your daggerboard when reaching and when running is frequently a difficult decision to make. As a general rule you go faster with it in place. However, if leaving it in will cause you to fall, or increases the risk of falling, then pull it up halfway or pull it out entirely. It is good to practice running and reaching in force-four winds and/or rough chop with your daggerboard down.

Pumping
Pumping is an important if somewhat gray area in boardsailing technique. A few pumps after each tack are generally considered essential and proper. Steady, rhythmic pumping at any time, however, is likely to earn you a protest.

Pumping really helps you along when sailing off the wind. There are two useful types of pumping action: (1) a fanning motion whereby the sail is tilted to leeward then brought quickly back to weather, and (2) a steering motion, especially good when you are on the run; pump-ing on the run involves moving the sail from side to side as if steering, changing the trim to give a positive angle of attack with each sideways movement—in fact, each time the board heads up or off it is accelerated.

Pumping is legal to promote planing, and therefore useful when marginal planing condi-tions exist. In such conditions concentrate very carefully on the water and give a pump whenever you think it will start you planing or surfing a wave. For example, just after a wave passes you by, give a strong pump to help the next wave catch you.

In lighter, smoother conditions pumping is not legal but the authors have noted that many racers find it so helpful that they search for ways to dis-guise their pumping. It all depends on how much pumping their competition is doing and whether they can get away with it. These racers find that subtle, infrequent steering, trimming and "losing balance" actions can give them enough speed to keep up with the leaders. In order that you can recognize pumping, figures 2 and 3 show what it looks like.

Mark rounding
The jibe and leeward marks can be particularly tricky to round. If you are in a crowd at the jibe mark you should probably use a push or power jibe in order to turn tightly and with control. If you have plenty of room a sharp semi-flare jibe is fastest.

At the leeward mark you have to be careful not to stall your sail or your daggerboard. Turning too sharply will stall the daggerboard and you will slip sideways. To turn smoothly and without stalling the sail, tilt the board to leeward slightly, tilt the sail as far as possible to leeward and let it luff just a little. You'll probably have difficulty heading up only if the wind is under 8 knots.

GO-FAST HINTS
Upwind
1. To counterbalance puffs in a light breeze, use your bottom. Rather than sheeting out momen-tarily or extending your arms, try bending at the waist just a bit to cope with the increased pull.

For bigger puffs you'll have to stick your bottom out and extend your arms, but only sheet out if an actual gust threatens to pull you over.

Fig. 2A *Pumping with fanning motion*

Fig. 2B

Fig. 3A *Pumping on the run with steering motion*

Fig. 3B

Fig. 3C

Fig. 3D

2. In over 12 or 13 knots, that is, good solid wind for planing to windward, you must develop a technique for coping with waves while sailing upwind. The technique is a combination of steering through waves, adjusting sail trim, and weight movements. Head up a bit or give the sail a pump to get over a steep wave without losing speed. Bear off just a bit if the water ahead looks extra rough; point a little higher if you see a smoother patch. Sometimes when you are planing, particularly in smooth water, it pays to scallop to weather, that is, bear off a bit for speed then head up an extra bit to windward. Then before your speed dissipates from pointing too high, bear off again. To make this technique really work you must sheet in as you tilt your sail aft and thrust with your back foot. Bearing off again follows very closely.

3. The very flexible masts of most sailboards cause the sails to have a lot of twist. Thus it is frequently correct—particularly when using a full sail—to oversheet (sheet in a lot) the lower half of the sail so that the upper half is trimmed correctly.

4. Should you find yourself in the unfortunate position of going upwind in light air and chop you won't be able to do any of those fine-tuning things like scalloping and steering. You'll just have to point high and slog through the chop. It'll seem terribly slow, but bearing off a bit for more speed doesn't help.

5. It's no good trying to trim your sail so that it pulls hardest on your arms. Maximum pull does not mean maximum lift. Always remember to keep your sail on the verge of luffing for maximum lift.

Downwind

The downwind legs are even more important with sailboards than with other planing boats. The surfing and planing capabilities of sailboards make for incredible potential differences in speed, particularly in marginal planing conditions. Each time you start surfing or planing you probably double your speed.

1. Always keep your bow headed into a trough—the biggest trough you can find.

2. When catching a wave, keep your eye on the wave ahead. If you try to keep up with the wave just ahead, the one behind is sure to catch you.

3. If you are surfing a wave and it is about to pass you by, head up a bit to maintain speed and prepare to catch the next wave, or else you'll be left wallowing and with no speed to catch it.

4. Although a higher angle of sail on a reaching leg is usually faster than a lower angle, there are frequently times when the chop is so big and the wind so light that the lower point of sail is faster because of a wave pattern which allows you to continuously surf by heading down across waves, instead of up across waves. You can use this knowledge to pass someone to leeward on a reach.

STARTING

The most popular method of starting in a large fleet (over 30 boards) is by "parking" on the starting line, drifting toward the port end, and then sheeting in at the gun. The sailboard's rapid acceleration and great maneuverability allow this technique to work.

If the starboard end of the line is favored there's likely to be a dense crowd at that end. It is safest to look for a gap in the line just to leeward of the crowd, but you can try for a perfect start if you want to risk getting knocked down or trapped behind someone else who has fallen. Rather than sail, try to "drift" with the crowd to the starboard end of the line, carefully estimating your rate of movement so that you arrive there just before the gun goes off.

In very light winds (under 5 knots) you must establish your position in the crowd early on in the sequence. But in stronger winds, gaps open and close constantly and you can afford to lay back a bit, spot a gap and fill it just before the gun. The danger in this is that the gap may close suddenly. You must weigh this against the advantage of speed as you cross the line at the gun.

One additional hint: if it is windy stay away from people who are likely to drop a sail on your head 5 seconds before the gun.

TACTICS AND STRATEGY

The necessity for tactics and strategy makes sailboard racing an intellectual activity. Tactics is the art of maneuvering to gain positional advantage over opponents. This calls for thorough knowledge of the rules and ability to wring advantage from application of these rules whenever two or more boats encounter each other. Strategy, on the other hand, is the art of developing a master plan for a race, e.g. whether to take the left side of the beat, whether to expect and plan for a persistent wind shift during the run, whether the current should be considered.

With a poorly finished daggerboard you can lose a few feet per leg. But with poor tactics you can lose a few boat lengths per leg, while with poor strategy you can lose a third of the leg. That's why it is so important to study some good books on the tactics and strategy of dinghy racing (the differences between these aspects of racing sailboards and conventional dinghies being relatively few and unimportant).

Among all other considerations, though, temper your decisions with the rule, "it is better to go slowly in the right direction than quickly in the wrong direction."

LONG-DISTANCE RACING

The long-distance race is a popular event at Windsurfer regattas, drawing hundreds of competitors to race the course which is usually between 8 and 15 miles long. In Hawaii 15- 30-mile marathon races are held frequently, but only in winds over force 4.

The Le Mans start is often used. Boards and rigs are placed at the water's edge, some carefully, some haphazardly, all too close together. The contestants stand in a line parallel to the shore, 50 to 100 feet from the shore, and at the gun scramble madly for their boards. The object is to set sail quickly without being tripped by a mast or skegged in the back.

One way to start successfully is to find a spot surrounded by less cutthroat sailors so you can get the jump on them. Rules don't count for much in Le Mans starts, so if you want to win you have to "duke it out."

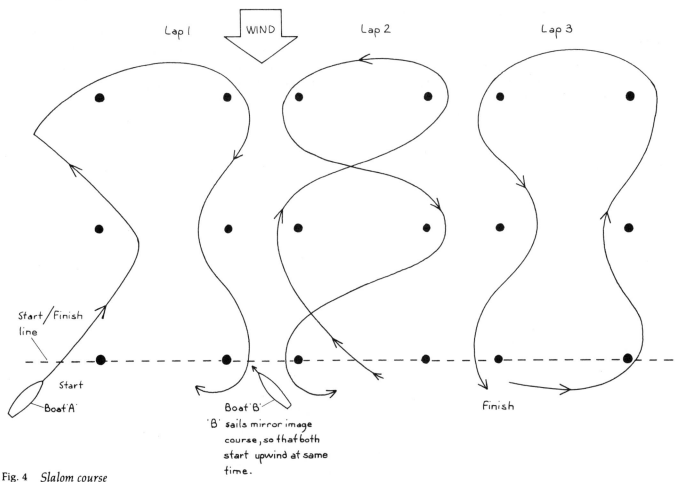

Fig. 4   *Slalom course*

Pure speed is tested in races with mostly reaches, whereas ability to pick the major wind shifts is important where there is a long beat. Pumping ability and good sail adjustment also make a big difference.

SLALOM

Slalom racing is a real test of boat handling ability as well as speed, particularly in strong winds. In fact, in winds of less than 10 knots slalom tends to be a little boring, whereas in over 15 knots it is extremely demanding for contestants and very exciting for spectators.

Competitors are usually matched in pairs in a single or double elimination ladder, and race one-on-one over a course such as the popular example in fig. 4. A longer, more demanding course is set up permanently near the town of St. Francis on the Caribbean island of Guadaloupe.

To excel at slalom you must have a fast tack, be able to perform the four major types of jibe (and variations) perfectly, and have a good memory, as many of the courses are complicated.

ATTITUDE

A winning frame of mind is probably the single most important attribute of a successful skipper. It consists of three things: (1) a desire to win, (2) a belief that you can win, and (3) the mental discipline (concentration) to win.

If you are a good loser, if you don't regard it as a personal insult and moral outrage to finish back in the pack, you don't have sufficient desire to win.

It is imperative you keep a high opinion of yourself (and keep it to yourself) and that you expect to be in at the top. If you don't expect to be with the winners, you won't be.

In the last analysis, as Matt Schweitzer has written in *Windsurfer Magazine* (Summer 1978, Vol. 8, No. 1), "Concentration is the name of the game." You must concentrate while sailing by yourself, while practicing with others, and while in a race. Your concentration shouldn't be a teeth-clenching "CONCENTRATE" sort of thing. Rather it should be complete absorption in the information your mind is receiving, e.g. the tug of the boom in your hands, the feel of the board under your feet, the approach of that starboard tack boat ahead, the darkening of the water just upwind.

When racing seriously you mustn't waste energy cursing someone who fouls you, and you can't afford the luxury of berating yourself for hitting a mark. You have to stay calm, shut out emotions such as hatred, anger, love, joy, disgust and satisfaction, and direct all your resources to sensing, interpreting and acting upon information which can help you sail the fastest course.

You must have so much desire to win that you momentarily hate the person covering you, you have to have so much confidence that you exult in competition, and you must have so much mental discipline that your concentration is not broken by these emotions.

SURF AND WAVE SAILING

11

Boardsailing in surf is the sport at its best—this is "wind-surfing" in the literal sense, and for many of the sport's top practitioners has become the ultimate challenge.

No other aspect of boardsailing, and perhaps no other sport, harnesses as many sources of energy. The force of gravity, the power of a wave and the velocity of the wind combine to produce a very high-energy pastime. But more than that, no other aspect of boardsailing demands as much physical skill as, for example, landing from a 40-foot jump; nor as much experience, judgment and concentration as necessary to put oneself on a teetering 15-foot wall of water. No other aspect of boardsailing demands as much ingenuity in developing equipment that will perform satisfactorily. And nothing else in the sport returns as much excitement and satisfaction.

As Larry Stanley has said, "The essence of surfing . . . is the free-falling super-speeding gravity-pulling wave-rushing feeling of being on a vertical face. And in windsurfing that's accentuated because you've got twice the speed. You have motive force other than gravity and the wave."*

CONDITIONS
Types of waves
It is wise to know a little about waves before risking your mast in them.

The type of wave most people do their wind-surfing in is called "windwave," or "chop." Windwaves are generated by the local wind and

---

*From an interview with Larry Stanley, Appendix.

Note:
In this chapter the term "surfing" refers to boardsailing in breaking waves.

in deep water are characterized by short wavelengths (distance between wave peaks) and steep faces, as illustrated in figure 1D. Breaking windwaves that are greater than head height tend to line up somewhat, to form fairly long peaks, but those less than head height show very little regularity or predictability. If you're surfing windwaves you'll find that the farther you get from the beach, the larger they are, but the less powerfully and frequently they break.

The type of wave that we see surfers in Hawaii riding is part of what is called a "ground swell," or just "swell." A ground swell is generated by the wind of a storm hundreds of miles from the reef or shore on which it breaks. Although the swell starts out as gigantic windwaves in a storm, by the time it has traveled a thousand miles it will have subsided to an innocuous-looking undulation (see fig 1B). However, when this undulation approaches land and shallow water, it increases in height and steepness until, upon breaking, it has doubled in height. Swells make for the best surfing. They form long, continuous peaks and break in a predictable manner.

How waves break
When a wave breaks over a gradually shoaling seabed it rolls. That is, it peaks up and gradually gets higher and steeper until it finally breaks at the top in a tumbling fashion (fig. 1E). This tumbling continues until the wave reaches either deeper water or the shore. Rolling waves (mushers) are relatively gentle and easy to learn surfing on.

At the opposite end of the spectrum are "plungers," waves which break over a steep beach or shelf or any seabed that shoals rapidly over a

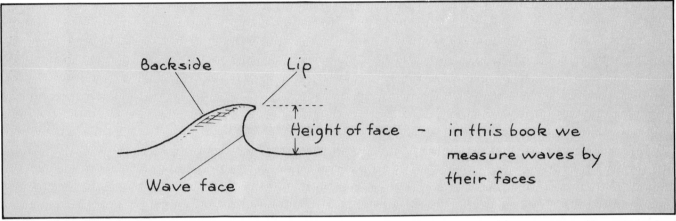

Fig. 1A   *The makeup of a wave*

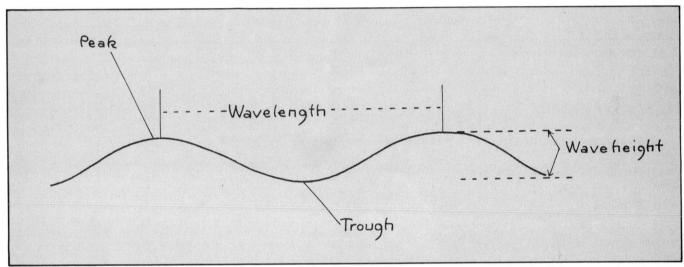

Fig. 1B   *Swell: nonbreaking waves in deep water*

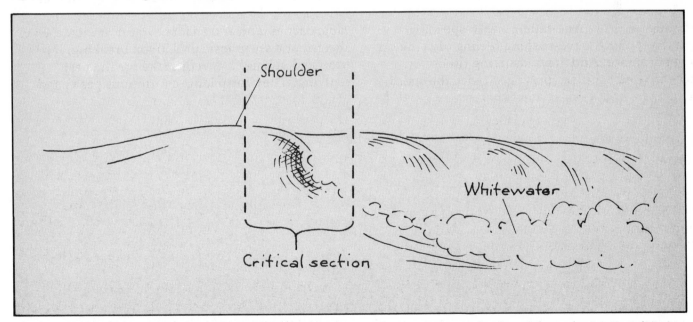

Fig. 1C   *The wave breaks from the left to the right of the person riding it. Therefore we say it is breaking right, or that it is "a right"*

Fig. 1D *Windwaves*

Fig. 1E *Mushy roller*

Fig. 1F *Hollow plunger*

short distance. Plungers peak up to maximum height very quickly, then break from top to bottom, forming a tube of water (fig. 1F). The entire force of this type of wave is expended in a moment, thus making it particularly dangerous.

Wind is another factor that affects how a wave breaks. An offshore wind, one which is blowing into the face of a wave, will tend to make the wave hollower and make it stand higher and longer before it breaks. An onshore wind tends to push a wave down, make it mushy and make it break prematurely.

For more useful terminology relating to waves, see figure 1A and C.

Wind strength and direction

There are five distinct directions from which the wind can come relative to the direction of travel of the waves (fig. 2). Note that waves usually break parallel to the shore.

Wind directions between 3 and 4 are the best for your first experiences in surf. The word "dead" in directions 1 and 5 is apt because that's what you may be if you try to learn in those conditions. Once you are experienced, all directions except for 1 can be excellent, depending on other variables such as wind strength, wave size, wave type, distance of the break from shore, etc.

Wakes

One type of wave that shouldn't be overlooked is the type generated by powerboats. Lake sailors who are a little bored with flat water can surf and jump wakes with no problem. Big (50-foot) planing hulls throw up the best wakes when they are going at just under planing speed. The biggest

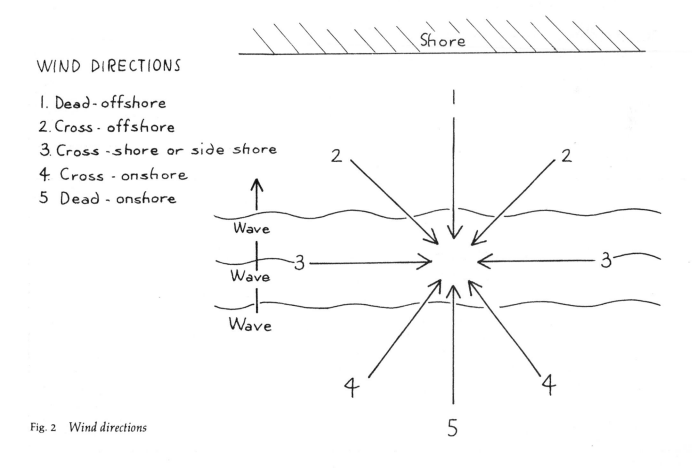

Fig. 2 *Wind directions*

and steepest waves are within 30 feet of the stern of the boat. Figure 3 illustrates a good setup.

Look out for boats trailing fishing lines, and be sure not to accidentally jump aboard like a flying fish.

SURFING

For the first few months or years, depending on how often you go out, you needn't worry about getting the latest in radical new surfing gear. You're liable to break it faster than you can buy it.

This chapter discusses the type of surfing available to people who live near a large body of water and own a Windsurfer-type board. The shape of the Windsurfer is that of an old-fashioned surfboard, a fact which makes it excellent for surfing. The Windsurfer's very flexible mast, though not very fast, doesn't break easily in surf—another good point. So if you've made the modifications and have the equipment listed below and discussed in chapter 6, you are already well equipped to handle pretty gnarly conditions.

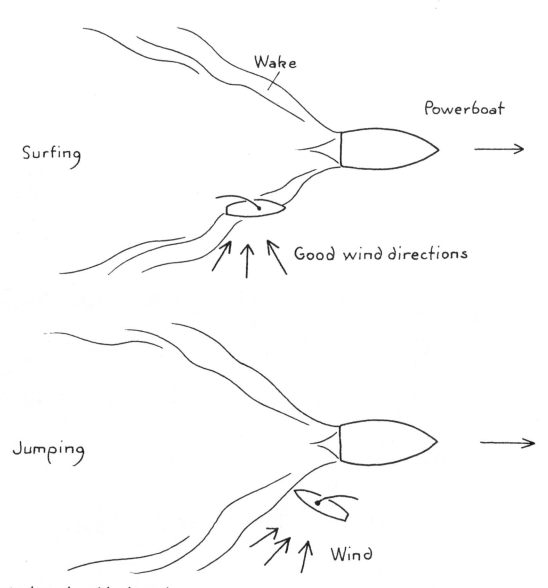

Fig. 3   *Powerboat wakes can be surfed and jumped*

Surfing Equipment

Surfboard-type board
  —no "V" bottom.
  —10- or 12-inch scoop.
  —good nonskid surface.
  —no sharp deck contours or seams.
  —soft (round) rails everywhere except perhaps
    the aft 3 or 4 feet.
Flexible fiberglass mast.
Aluminum booms.
Surfing/high-wind daggerboard.
Assorted skeg sizes.
Battenless straight leech sail with raised clew.
Leash.

The section on strapboards and sophisticated rigs, later in this chapter, will take you to expert level.

Site selection

Careful site selection will aid your first efforts in the surf. The wind should be 10 to 12 knots, sideshore or cross-onshore, and 2- to 3-foot waves should be breaking on a sandbar or reef at least 100 feet from shore. There should be only surges hitting the beach, no breaking waves, otherwise you'll be unable to even get off the beach. The waves should be the rolling type, not plungers.

Launching

Method 1
For launching where the shore break isn't rough (in Oklahoma, for example) it is hard to beat this flashy Hawaiian method. You hold the board as illustrated and push it into the water. If the beach is steep, you can push the board into the water and step on without even getting your feet wet— for whatever that's worth.

Fig. 4   *Launch method 1*

Fig. 5A *Launch method 2*

Fig. 5B

Fig. 5C

Fig. 5D

Fig. 5E

Method 2
Slightly different from the widely practiced "rig in one hand, board in the other" method illustrated in chapter 1, this method was developed for launching in rough shore break. It allows you to get on the board more quickly and without dropping the sail into the water. It's important that you not drop your rig; even a small wave can snap your mast before you can say "One Hundred Dollars."

Fig. 6A   *Launch method 3*

Fig. 6B

Fig. 6C

Method 3

For a really impractical but flashy way to launch, try a beach start. That is, sail your board across the sand into the water with the daggerboard hanging on your arm. To sail in bow first requires removing your skeg—which isn't too smart because you won't be able to sail once you're in the water. It's better to go stern first; that way you can keep the skeg from digging into the sand. Once on the water, do a hull 180°, drop your daggerboard in and sail away.

Landing

Landing is considerably easier than launching, since you are going in the same direction as the waves. Simply sail toward shore until you touch bottom or are about to touch, hold the mast with your forward hand, step off beside the board, lift the stern with your back hand and push it up the beach.

You should know from your experiences launching how rapidly the water shoals near shore and whether it is safe for your feet to hop

Fig. 7A

Fig. 7B *Landing*

off into the water. If there are waves breaking right on the beach, land by following closely behind a big wave so that you can sail up the beach a way on the surge.

GOING OUT
Surges
Once you've successfully launched you are faced with the problem of getting through masses of surging whitewater. This problem is particularly severe when the seabed slopes very gradually and the waves are windwaves; you may have to punch through six or eight surges of whitewater on the way out. If the wind is sideshore the surges shouldn't be too troublesome, because you can sail straight through them. But if the wind is cross-onshore you'll have to sail the course shown in figure 8.

Head up into each surge to punch through, then bear off to gain enough speed and momentum to punch through the next surge. Should your board be sideways to the surge you'll probably be knocked down, or at least carried shoreward a considerable distance. Should you fall, get the sail out of the water as quickly as possible. If you can stand on the bottom, hold the mast over your head out of the water.

You'll find that running into a surge is almost like running aground; the board stops suddenly, but you don't. Be ready for it by shifting your weight to your back foot just before hitting the surge.

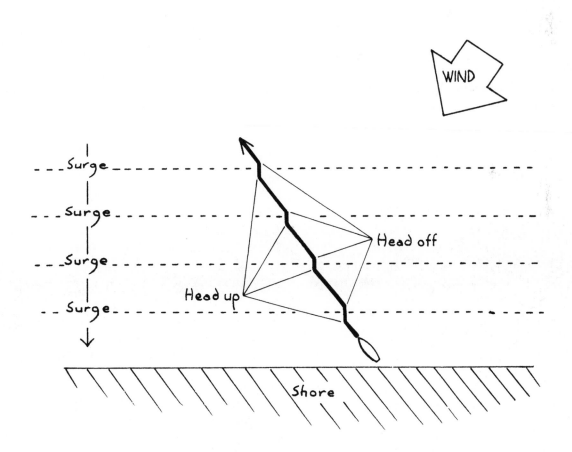

Fig. 8   *Sailing out through surges of whitewater*

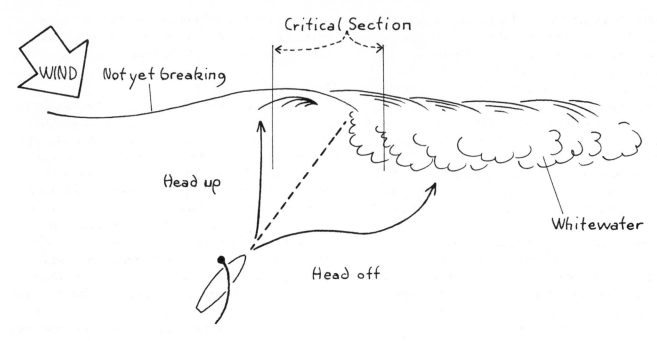

Fig. 9 *Head up or head off to avoid reaching a wave as it breaks*

Peaks

After you've gone through one or two or possibly more surges, you'll face a wave that is about to break. Try not to get to it just as it breaks (critical section), because that is when it is most powerful. Get to it a second before or a second after it breaks. If you can't do that, head up or off toward a less critical section, one that has already broken or one that has yet to break (fig. 9). Only experience will enable you to judge and time your approach to breaking waves properly.

You needn't worry too much about heading up as you approach a peak. Just concentrate on keeping your weight back and be prepared to luff if necessary. You'll feel a brief weightless thrill as you drop down the back of the wave. Enjoy it—it's an appetizer.

Jumps

Once you are experienced enough to go out in 3-foot waves and 15 knots of wind you'll be able to do some wave jumping. To get airborne, you'll need to head up the steepest part of the wave, but you have to get there before it breaks. Again, experience and timing are very important.

You'll also want to have the maximum possible speed, so head off to your fastest course, then

head as near directly perpendicular to the wave as possible. When going up the wave, crouch a little and shift your weight to your back foot. Push down with your back foot so that it remains in contact with the board as you leave the water. Luff your sail to keep the board from turning over, then sheet in and head off as you land.

No matter how windy and rough it is, you won't be able to get more than a few inches or a foot out of the water and still retain control. However, if you don't mind losing control the sky's the limit. You can sail full speed in a 25-knot wind into a 10-foot wave just to see how high you can get. Be sure to let go your booms, though, so the wind can blow your board away, or you may fall 15 feet onto a skeg.

COMING IN
Onshore wind

Your first concern upon finding yourself safely beyond the breakers should be getting safely back to shore. So at first don't worry about picking a big wave and getting radical; just try to ride an ordinary wave all the way in without falling.

Starting well outside where the waves are breaking, sail toward shore. You'll soon catch, or rather be caught by a wave that will increase your speed considerably. Head straight down the wave until you start to outrun it. Then head up to traverse the face. Keep an eye on the section of wave just in front of you. If it gets very steep and appears about to break, bear off sharply down the face. Bearing off down a wave is a little more tricky than bearing off in flat water. On the wave you must not only tilt the sail forward, but also tilt your leeward rail down.

Once down and in front of the wave, you don't have to worry when it breaks. Just outrun it until the surge of whitewater subsides, then tack back out.

If you have to surf in a place where the surges are strong right to the beach, you'll have to kick out of the wave before the section in front of you breaks. To do this, head up sharply by stepping back and weighting the windward rail as soon as the section you are on becomes critical. As the wave swirls by and breaks you'll have to tack immediately and quickly so as not to be taken by surprise when the next one approaches.

Be conservative until you gain experience. Stay near the top of a wave if you are going to kick out before it breaks. Stay low in it if you plan to run in front of it.

As you become comfortable in surf you'll want to make more turns on the waves and stay closer to the critical sections. A small skeg allows you to make tight quick turns with just the flick of a leg. You'll progress to bigger, steeper waves, also. On a steep face you have to weight your windward rail a lot in order to head up the wave. Conversely, if you want to head down a steep hollow face, tilt your leeward rail down a lot.

In general, stay out of the whitewater, but if you get caught sideways by a surge, just squat down, get your weight over the board and sheet in. If you start to fall to leeward, back the sail. With luck you won't fall.

Sideshore wind
Sideshore wind conditions are similar to onshore except that with a sideshore wind you can easily go right or left on a wave. You can catch a wave while beam reaching, head off to traverse it on a broad reach, then cut back to close-hauled going the other way. When broad reaching you'll have to weight the leeward rail in order to head up the wave; just tilting the sail forward isn't enough.

When beam reaching or close-hauled on the wave, you can luff your sail or even back it for steering and slowing purposes.

Cross-offshore wind
Cross-offshore wind is usually accompanied by a smooth, hollow ground swell type of wave and permits outrageous speeds. With the wind going one way and the wave going the other (fig. 10), the surfer is like a watermelon seed squeezed between the thumb and forefinger of God and then shot out at the devil.

In these conditions you'll find you are close-hauled all the time because the more you head off, the faster you go and the farther forward your apparent wind shifts. You'll also find that heading off is even more difficult than before. For example, when you drop down the wave and try to head off to traverse it you must simultaneously hike out, sheet in, tilt the sail forward and to windward *and* tilt the leeward rail down. It's the last part that's tricky, and the steeper the wave the harder it is to do.

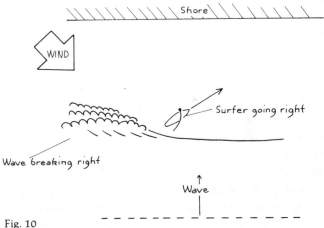

Fig. 10

A cross-offshore wind and smooth, hollow ground swell waves permit outrageous speeds

Be wary of the gusts and lulls that are likely to be present in an offshore wind. And if the waves are big, over 10 feet, you'll find that the wind swirls and eddies behind the waves, while in front it is extra strong and steady.

MANEUVERS
Tack
The type of tack to use in rough water is method 1 in chapter 4. If you've learned it well and can do

it in flat water, rough water shouldn't give you too much trouble.

When going out with sideshore or onshore winds, just concentrate on starting your tack as you go up a swell and finishing it after the peak passes.

Coming in you'll find that you can use your tremendous speed and the force of the breaking wave to power an amazingly fast tack. When the section of wave in front of you appears to be about to break, and you've decided to tack, tilt your sail back and push with your back foot as if to tack normally, but push only for a second. If your timing is good and the wave is about to break, all you have to worry about is getting to the other side of the sail. The peak of the wave will take care of turning the board. With practice you'll be able to tack and sheet in before the board stops planing.

Running jibe
If you are using a 3- or 4-inch skeg and high-wind daggerboard in over 15 knots of wind you should be able to turn quickly by doing a high-speed running jibe. Head off normally with the sail tilted to weather and tilt the windward rail down slightly by moving your forward foot aft a bit and putting more weight on it. As you approach a downwind course, shift your weight entirely to the new back foot, lean into your turn and step forward with your new front foot. During this forward step your back foot controls the banking of the board and thus your rate of turn; banking into the turn will slow your rate of turn and vice versa. This last action also serves to shove the tail of the board around so that by the time you've shifted your feet you are sailing by the lee. Complete the maneuver by immediately letting the sail swing around.

If you have a large skeg you can still jibe quickly, but not with quite as much speed over the water as in the previous case. You'll need to tilt the sail and your board to windward as described above, but you also have to step back on the board a foot or two as you head off. Don't step back so much that you slow down a lot, as in the flare jibe, but

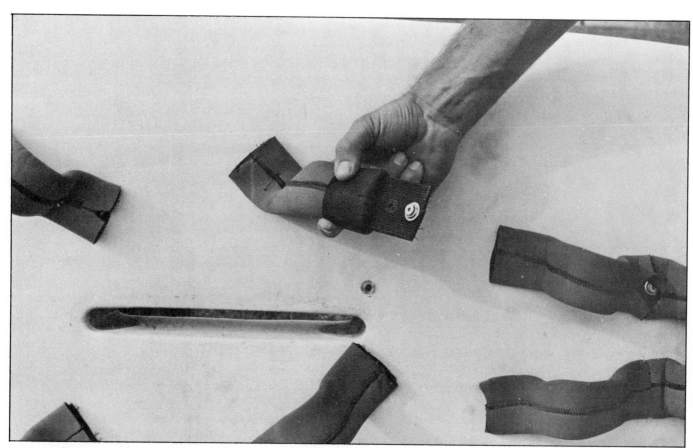

Fig. 11A   *Footstrap made of seatbelt-type webbing covered with neoprene*

nevertheless move back enough to cause the board to turn on its tail.

These jibes are particularly fast and exciting when done on the faces of waves. When going out with a cross-onshore wind, look for a steep but not yet breaking peak. Head off as you go up it and complete your jibe as you reach the peak. The wave will allow you to turn very quickly, and since you'll be dropping down the face, you'll accelerate out of the jibe.

HIGH-PERFORMANCE WINDSURFING
With the advent of footstraps a whole new set of techniques and capabilities came to boardsailing. Straps give greater control, allowing greater speeds and making for a more spectacular, exciting sport. Below is a brief discussion of the equipment that is part of this revolution.

Straps
Straps usually consist of a piece of seatbelt-type webbing covered with 3/16-inch neoprene. The neoprene, which has a layer of thin nylon on it, is often sewn or glued to the webbing. In the case of the Windsurfer Rocket, the neoprene is sewn into a tube 1½ inch in diameter and slipped over the webbing (fig. 11A).

There are two main ways of attaching the webbing to the deck. One way is to fiberglass it on permanently. The other way is to use threaded inserts, which are embedded in the board and to which the straps are screwed. This second method allows adjustment of the straps for different foot sizes and makes initial attachment of the straps easier.

The placement of straps is a very personal thing. Light people need them near the windward rail, heavy people prefer them in the middle of the deck. The sizes and locations of skegs and daggerboards also affect where the straps go. Figure 11B shows a good all-around arrangement.

Boards
Once you've graduated from your standard Windsurfer or other basic, general-purpose sailboard you'll find a wide variety of more

Fig. 11B *Strap placement on a Windsurfer Rocket*

sophisticated boards from which to choose. There are the long, single-skeg racing strapboards such as the Naish/Mistral. There is the Windsurfer Rocket, good (but not ideal) for racing, jumping and surfing, and there are the short, maneuverable, low-buoyancy, high-speed boards designed strictly for surfing and jumping.

The best boards for jumping and surfing are small (8 to 11 feet long), for quick turning and for low windage when airborne. They are designed to carve turns after the fashion of surfboards, and must be constructed of materials such as Kevlar (an aramid fiber by Du Pont), Klegecell foam (a polyvinylchloride foam) and carbon fibers, in order to withstand the stress of jumping.

The Windsurfer Rocket is a good board for your first sorties into high-performance windsurfing because of its relative low cost, versatility and ruggedness. And since it is the most widely used strapboard, the following discussion of technique will apply specifically to that board.

Sails

Small changes and gradual improvements in the sails used in Hawaii are reflected in the sails sewn by Pat Love of Kailua.

These generally have a lot of luff curve for good shape in strong winds. The boom opening allows booms to be up to 6 feet above the deck. (High booms allow you more leverage over the sail.) Large windows permit you to see the wave you are on. And, very important, the clews are 1 to 2 feet higher than those on most standard sails, so that they don't drag in the water.

More and more of the top sailors are using higher aspect ratio (HAR) rigs. On high aspect ratio rigs the booms are shorter and masts are taller. A typical HAR storm sail might have, instead of an 11-foot luff and 9-foot booms, a 14-foot luff and 7-foot booms. There are three main advantages associated with HAR rigs: (1) they are more efficient at high speeds, (2) their center of effort doesn't shift as radically when they luff, and (3) the clew doesn't drag in the water. One disadvantage is that they require stiffer, more expensive, more easily broken masts.

Getting into your straps

When you are new to strapboards you usually have to watch your feet in order to get them into the correct footstraps. Meanwhile an unexpected gust of wind hits and puts you off balance.

Use of the following procedure at least reduces the chance of your being catapulted while fumbling for the straps:

1. Don't hook in with your harness.
2. Keep your front foot well forward.
3. Slip your back foot into a strap.
4. Slip your front foot into a strap.
5. Sheet in and go.
6. Hook in with the harness.

Again, it is a matter of personal preference which straps you use, but as a general rule the forward straps are used for windward work, the aft straps for reaching.

Be sure your straps are the right size. If they're too small they are useless; too large, they are dangerous. You can sprain or break a foot or ankle by getting it jammed in a strap that is too large.

To keep your feet in the straps, try curling the toes down on your back foot. The toes on the front foot should curl up.

Jumping

Keep in mind that you can hurt yourself jumping with footstraps, so use maximum caution.

Don't jump with your harness hooked in, and at first go into jumps slowly and with control. Luff the sail and tilt it forward as you leave the top of a wave, just as you did without straps. Luffing keeps you from going too high; tilting forward keeps you from heading up.

Use your back foot to push the tail down and keep the board flat while airborne. Don't try to jump more than a couple of feet if you can't keep from dropping the leeward rail. And strive for soft tail-first landings, because they're the safest for you and your board (see color insert).

Once you've mastered small jumps, luffing the sail and with tail-first landings, and can avoid heading up or dropping the rail, you can proceed to "flying jumps."

Approach the wave normally but shift your weight way back and squat a little. As you leave the water lock your legs and keep the sail sheeted in. This action normally allows a good high jump with a safe landing (see color insert).

Here are some hints on what to do in the air:

1. In soft tail-first landings push your back

foot down. For flat fast landings pull your back foot up.

2. To avoid heading up, tilt the sail forward and/or sheet in.

3. To head off in the air, tilt the windward rail up so that the wind blows the bow downwind, and tilt the sail to windward. Level out before landing.

4. To get maximum air (height), crouch as you go up the face, then spring up as you leave the lip.

5. If you hit a peak just as it's lipping over and end up doing a half gainer—that is, the board keeps going up until it's over the top of you and your mast is pointing toward the water—BAIL OUT. Kick the board away (the wind will carry it away from you) and curl into a ball for safe splashdown.

One last word of advice. Keep in mind how painful it is to do an incomplete flip and bellyflop into the water from the 10-foot diving board, and consider that there will be frequent occasions when you are bailing out from higher than that.

Surfing

On a Rocket you can do everything you can do on a Windsurfer, plus a lot more. One basic difference between the two, however, is in the way they turn. On the Windsurfer you bank the board to the left to turn to the right, but on the Rocket you bank into your turn, cutting the inside rail into the water and carving a turn. The difference arises because the center of lateral resistance (mainly comprised of daggerboard and skegs) is farther aft on the Rocket, thus permitting it to turn on its tail rather than around its daggerboard as the Windsurfer does.

What this means is that with the Rocket you have a board which is directionally stable, yet easy to turn by banking.

The footstraps make handling whitewater much easier, both going out and coming in. In fact, if you are on a mushy wave you can drop down a breaking peak right in the whitewater and your feet won't get washed off the board.

Straps also allow perhaps the ultimate wave maneuver—surfing and jumping at the same time. With a wind direction between 4 and 5 (fig. 2), catch a wave and surf it. Then when the section in front of you gets steep, cut up the face of the wave. If you maintain good speed you can

jump into the air, head off and drop back down to surf the same wave.

There are hundreds of different moves to do in surf, depending on the conditions, your equipment, your ability and your imagination.

Jibing

You can not only carve turns with a Rocket, you can carve jibes.

Starting from a beam reach on starboard (for example) in a solid 15 knots of wind or more, your right foot should be in the aft of the two forward straps. Step to leeward near the aftmost strap with your left foot, tilt the sail to windward and bank to the left by lifting the heel of your right foot. Don't bank too much or you'll turn too sharply; just keep the hull at a uniform angle for a smooth carving turn. Just after your stern passes the eye of the wind, transfer your weight entirely to your back foot, which will maintain the angle of the bank since it is on the left side of the board, and step way back with your right foot. Now simultaneously or in quick succession step forward with your left foot (placing it in the appropriate strap) and let the sail swing around. The hardest part of the jibe is figuring out how far to lean into the turn. The faster you are going and the harder you are banking, the more you lean. If someday somebody mistakes you for a slalom water-skier, you'll know you're doing it right.

COMPETITION

Wave-oriented competition started quite early in the history of windsurfing. Matt Schweitzer was winning subjective wave-riding contests back in 1974. However it wasn't until early 1980 that serious competition got going. There had been earlier attempts (the Hawaii World Cups of 1978 and 1979 had no wind) but nothing on the scale of the professional and amateur events organized at the start of this decade.

The two main events are the subjective wave riding and jumping competition, and the objective "ins and outs" race.

The subjective event calls for judges to evaluate the performance of the contestant in categories such as:

1. Number of falls.
2. Number of jumps and rides.
3. Height of jumps.
4. Control in jumps.
5. Maneuvers entering, exiting and while riding on exciting waves.
6. Ability to stay in the critical section.

Flat-water tricks such as railrides and duckspin tacks are superfluous and undesirable in this type of competition.

The "ins and outs" race is strictly objective. Heats of four to six sailors race through the course shown in figure 12 in high wind and surf. The top one or two finishers of each heat then proceed to another heat, and so on.

DANGERS

To get the most enjoyment out of your surfing you must be aware of the risks involved:

1. Look out for sharks—don't be paranoid, but don't dawdle when it comes to getting back on your board.

2. Look out for surfers. They don't have such sharp teeth as sharks do, but they probably have more tough friends on the shore. So don't hog all the waves or pass surfers too closely.

3. In a tropical area, if you get cut on coral, or anything else for that matter, treat the wound with a topical antiseptic ointment such as Neosporin so that you don't get a "staph" infection.

4. Don't go out in waves over head height unless you are a good swimmer. You're sure to be separated from your board sooner or later.

5. Longshore drift, the current parallel to the shore caused by the breaking waves, can be very strong. Don't get swept downwind.

6. Rip currents, which result from the wave action, are always seabound and can carry your board and rig out to sea.

7. In a wipeout on a big wave, the safest place to be is 10 feet underwater. If surfers can be killed by being hit with a 10-pound board, just think what a 40-pound board can do.

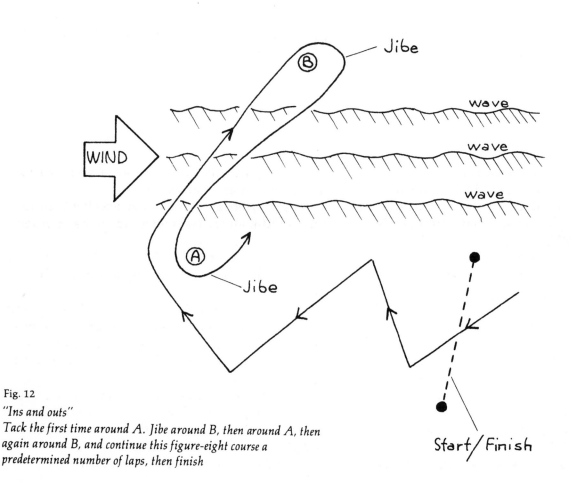

Fig. 12

"Ins and outs"
Tack the first time around A. Jibe around B, then around A, then again around B, and continue this figure-eight course a predetermined number of laps, then finish

WINDSURFING-WANDERING

12

To add to the many windsurfing locations you'll discover near your home, here are a few interesting spots with good wind and, all except San Francisco, water over 21°C. (70°F.). When you consider some of these locations you may wish that air travel could be made free as well as the wind. If you don't work for an airline or have another such job that's ideal for windsurfing-wandering, you may be inspired to save your shekels to visit these places. Warm water and ideal wind make the sport glorious. To feel at harmony with the elements—that's what windsurfing is all about.

NORTH AMERICA

Buzzards Bay, New England has excellent and reliable summer thermals frequently exceeding 20 knots from the southwest. There is a strong fleet of excellent racers in the area.

Cape Hatteras, North Carolina has warm water from May to October, excellent storms and super waves. People also say that Wrightsville Beach, north of Wilmington, is a superb place with fine waves and wind and a long sandy beach with good access and a quick drop-off in depth— but watch for a strong current.

Florida's east coast south of Cape Canaveral rivals Hawaii for warm water, strong winds and big waves in winter months. These same conditions apply in the Bahamas.

The south Texas coast along the Gulf of Mexico is warm from May to October, and has 15 to 20 knots of wind out of the southeast most summer days. Maximum water temperature is about 30°C. (85°F.).

San Francisco Bay is never as warm as you'd like (maximum about 18°C.) but has some of the best summer winds in North America. A thermal wind well over 20 knots whistles through the Golden Gate most summer afternoons.

California also has numerous lakes with excellent wind. The San Luis reservoir near Los Banos is windier than San Francisco, and warmer too. Lake Lopez near San Luis Obispo also has an excellent summer thermal. And the surf spot called Zeros, just south of Leo Carrillo State Beach, has probably the best summer wind and waves in all southern California.

OTHER LOCATIONS

Baja in Mexico has good wind, warm water, and waves on the ocean side, flat water on the Sea of Cortez.

Cancun, Mexico can have good winter winds and both surf and flat water.

Most Caribbean islands have excellent spring winds (20-knot trades) and good winds at other times.

Brazil is reputed to have conditions which rival Hawaii year round—for example, at Cabo Frio, east of Rio de Janeiro.

In Europe, Lago di Garda in northern Italy, and Sardinia provide windy, warm summer weather, as do areas of the French Riviera such as the isle of Bendor. Porto Hydra, Greece is another windy spot.

Australia experiences strong thermal winds in the summer, has good waves—and plenty of sharks. Perth, particularly, is known for strong winds.

Hawaii is of course the Mecca of dedicated

boardsailors. Maui especially has remarkable wind because of its geography, but all the islands have consistent moderate summer trades and radical winter storms. You can find wind over 15 knots somewhere on Oahu two days out of three year round.

Needless to say, the waves in Hawaii are the best in the world, but there is also flat water.

Larry Stanley jumps a wave . . . then parachutes down with the sail horizontal. In such a maneuver the risks are high. For example, you may land on a skeg or daggerboard, or rip the sail with a skeg. According to Stan, "On the way down I keep the board away from myself by maintaining a hold on the booms and pushing on them if it looks like the board is going to land under me. In this instance it was a hard landing, but didn't really hurt. As much as anything, I was concentrating on parachuting to the water and didn't think to make a clean, soft entry. As a dive it would have got 3.2 out of 10."

APPENDIX

EVOLUTION OF WAVE JUMPING AND FOOT-STRAPS IN HAWAII

(An interview with Larry Stanley in the workshop of Windsurfing Hawaii, March 1979.)

Hawaii has influenced the world with its kind of high-performance windsurfing, and this interview records some major landmarks, including the origins of the Windsurfer Rocket.

INTERVIEWER: Roger Jones

STAN: Larry Stanley

INT: Stan, can we talk about what you recall of the evolution of wave jumping and the use of footstraps in Hawaii.

STAN: Thor (Michael Thor Horgan) started it. He came over with Andy Chaffee, both avid Windsurfer sailors transplanted from California. Thor's a very go-for-it person who windsurfs wherever he is, whatever conditions he finds. I was surfing when I first saw Thor. This was, I think, in 1972, '73. He taught me to windsurf and pretty soon we were crashing in waves together . . .

INT: When were footstraps first put on?

STAN: Well, personally I didn't keep a journal. But I think that in late 1976 or early '77 the first ones were put on for the purpose of controlling the Chip at high speeds—the Chip being the double-tunneled hull which the Windsurfer Star was patterned after. It's the one that's in the World Cup pictures and on the back of the Windsurfing Hawaii T-shirts. We

called it the Rocket Chip. The Chip was designed for stability and speed. Gary Seaman designed it and it was exactly like the Star (which came later) but smaller: 28 inches wide, 10 feet long, weighing about 36 to 38 pounds. Hoyle Schweitzer tried the Chip and didn't like it. He sold it to Andy Chaffee on one of Andy's trips to the mainland, and Andy brought it here. And we all went out and played with it and agreed it was fast, it was light, fairly floaty, kinda unstable, kinda funny to tack because when you jumped in front there was nothing there. But the daggerboard well was still right there next to the mast, way forward in the middle of the boat. And we couldn't get over the stability problems. So I started cutting it up and changing things on it. And trying to change the waterline somehow—just to make it more stable and not slip out. It appeared that there was just so much planing surface aft— take something square and it'll plane just as easily sideways as frontward. So you put some skegs there (aft)—well, they don't stop the sideways planing when they cavitate. The dumb thing, if you had the mast here and were going along on a beam reach or something, the back end would just slip right out on it and usually that would mean the nose would come round and hit you in the head. I started doing things, changing it, putting bigger skegs, and moved the daggerboard box aft, and cut some tail and made wings and stings and weird things. . . . Nothing worked. Thing still just skidded out. So instead of trying to figure out whatever under there, I knew the thing'd go fast, but I just couldn't stay on it when it got going, so I got some surfboard leash holders, the little inserts just like a little cup with a steel bar through it, and sank two there and two there and two in the back and tied webbing down and jammed my foot in and went out and sailed it—and it worked. You could keep the board straight . . . you could pull in with your foot, you could control it this way and you could keep the board going fast—faster than you could without straps.

It was a plateau. It still reached a point where it became uncontrollable even with footstraps. That was the original intention with footstraps—to be able to keep the Chip from spinning out at high speeds. Then we found it helped us control high jumps.

INT: Some people say straps were put on to keep your feet on in whitewater.

STAN: Footstraps were put on for what I told you. All the other stuff came because of it. It turned out that with footstraps you could go through whitewater well and you could control the board on the waves. But that wasn't the original intent. Patrick (Love)—he was the second person to put footstraps on, on his blue board, his first glass board, which was built a couple of years ago. It was a long time after footstraps were put on the Chip that they were put on anything else. I actually quit using the Chip after two or three weeks of playing with the footstraps because they were very uncomfortable and I was concentrating on learning new moves (for me) on my regular Windsurfer, and the Chip pearled really easily and wasn't that much fun on waves. So I shelved it for a long time. Then Pat got his blue board built and started going real fast again. But he still wasn't jumping it.

INT: When did the jumping start?

STAN: Thor and I were jumping '74, '75.

INT: Were you jumping and bailing out at that time?

STAN: We were going as high as we could on some. Some we'd bail out. That was fun for a couple of weeks. You can only get so high and bail out and crash so many different ways, on your back, on your neck, on your side, from these high jumps—on your board, your board on you. After a while it gets old, you know. You get tired of breaking things, of getting hurt and bruised. And you go to other things.

We'd left that. We'd done all that: going as high as we could and getting launched. And staying with it to the very top and flattening it out and then jumping off. And even staying on it sometimes. But you always hurt your feet, and your legs, and your board. So we quit.

And then we started getting into more controllable jumps. Going for distance. Without footstraps. We were still controlling the boards in the air with our feet. But then we started concentrating on picking the right ramp to give the most distance and speed. And the least amount of turbulence as you were going up the face. As you're going up the face of a wave that's breaking you can get a good jump with footstraps. Get up, just let the wind pick you up, and your momentum and the whitewater thrusting, and phsst! Get right in the air! But going up onto a face that has whitewater at the top, or an irregularity or a curve or a bowl or something, will throw your board off. And without footstraps it's difficult to compensate for that little twist or roll or whatever, as you go off the wave. So we were starting to get into picking our ramps. We were getting really good at seeing what kind of wave would give the right kind of ramp. And then we found that if you can keep the board flat the wind doesn't have as much influence on it. You could traject yourself 20, 50 feet; however far, I never measured. We started getting into that. And we were getting more and more into distance as opposed to height.

And then Jürgen (Hönscheid) came over from West Germany for the first Hawaiian World Cup (1978) and he was just going through that first phase: "Wow! In the air! It's neat." And like anyone else that discovers jumping they're going to try and go as high as they can and as far as they can. And they'll bail out at first.

Anyway, Jürgen was having a lot of fun with jumping, you know, rediscovering this thing, and was getting really high. And about this time Colin Perry was getting into jumping. And they went out and jumped a lot together. Well, Colin and Jürgen kinda rekindled the enthusiasm for jumping. And soon everyone was talking about these tremendously high jumps. Still bailing out—but so high in the air.

Well, you know, people are people, and egos are egos. And you go, Well, I can do that! I was doing that years ago. So you go out there, jumping and bailing out. It's the same old stuff. So I said, "Well, look. I've got this Chip I used last year which has footstraps. It's dumb not to use it for jumping." And that's when we started jumping first with footstraps, and discovering controlled flight.

INT: Was the Chip near ideal for jumping?

STAN: No. It's okay. But I don't consider any of the boards I've ever seen ideal for anything.

INT: So did you build a board for jumping?

STAN: No, I built my first yellow Go-kart because the others seemed too big. At the time there seemed no need for bigness if you're in an area where you're planing all the time, and in waves. One of the benefits of having a light short board is that it fits into waves really well. It also flies well. I'm sorry that I jumped that board and broke it before I had a Windsurfer Rocket, though. You can learn to land on a Rocket and you can't break it in half. You can make the landing real soft. It doesn't hurt your ankles and all that, and doesn't inhibit you like a glass board can.

INT: How did the Windsurfer Rocket get developed?

STAN: The first inkling that anything like that could be done was a conversation with Hoyle Schweitzer over the phone around 1976, '77. Thor and I were asking him to move the daggerboard well back. We couldn't get the daggerboards back as far as we felt they should be with the well where it was placed. The necks were getting so small we were running into difficulties as far as materials. We couldn't find anything strong enough that we could afford or was easy to use with a hacksaw and screwdriver, which was the extent of our workshop at the time. And we asked him, Can you move the well back. And he said that would be no problem.

But it wasn't till a year later that Colin Perry convinced Hoyle that he should build a Wind-surfer with relocated daggerboard well and mast steps, and put more leash (skeg) inserts on the deck for the purposes of attaching footstraps. So when Hoyle said he'd use an old mold I said, Oh boy! Couldn't believe it. Drew out a bunch of stuff. Measured the Chip, the yellow Go-kart, measured The Box (Thor's wood board), measured Pat Love's board, measured our modified Windsurfers. And finally went dot dot dot, draw draw, and that's where it came out. The first ones, the single-fin ones, only had a single set of front footstraps, and three back straps, and for the average person I'd say that's just about right. Even before we'd received the first single-front footstrap boards I thought we ought to put on a second set. They thought I should have got it right the first time. However, they made fifty of the single and we got them to put the second set of footstraps and then I wanted to move the back ones and have two sets about 2 inches either side of the centerline instead of one set along the centerline. And Hoyle said he'd put twin fins in. And it just came about because of Colin and Hoyle throwing it about, and me drawing where it should be, and altering it a couple of times, and them coming up with ideas like two skegs and plugging the original daggerboard well. At best it's still an interim measure.

INT: What's next for boardsailing?

STAN: I think surfing is more fun than jumping myself. Surfing the waves is just incredible. Jumping, well it's okay.

INT: You mean running through sets or staying with one wave?

STAN: Surfing in the surfing sense of the word. Staying with one wave. Being in the critical part of the wave, as close to vertical and free-falling as often as possible. The essence of surfing or skiing is the free-falling, super-speeding, gravity-pulling wave-rushing feeling of being on a vertical face. And in windsurfing that's accentuated because you've got twice the speed. You have motive force other than gravity and the wave.

GLOSSARY

ABEAM: at right angles to the centerline of the boat.

AFT: at, toward or near the stern or back of a boat.

BEAM REACH: sailing with wind abeam.

BEAR OFF (bear away): to alter course away from the wind (opp.—head up).

BEAT: the windward leg of course.

BEATING: sailing to windward close-hauled on alternate tacks.

BOW: the front end of a board or boat.

BROAD REACH: sailing with wind abaft of the beam.

CLOSE-HAULED: sailing as nearly as possible into the wind.

CLOSE REACH: point of sail between beam reach and close-hauled.

EYE OF THE WIND: the direction from which the true wind is blowing.

FORE: at, toward or near the bow or front end of a boat.

FORWARD: forward part of boat, near bow.

HEAD TO WIND: headed directly into the wind.

HEAD UP: to turn toward the wind (opp.—bear off).

JIBE (gybe): to change tacks by turning away from the wind, change tacks with the wind aft.

LEEWARD: downwind.

LUFF: (noun) the forward edge of a sail.
—(verb) (1) a sail luffs (U.K.: lifts) when wind strikes the leeward side of the sail ("back" of sail) near the luff.
(2) to bring head to wind.

OFF THE WIND: any course other than close-hauled.

ON THE WIND: close-hauled.

PEARL: a board pearls when the nose drops enough to dig in and slow or stop the board.

PORT: left side of boat when looking forward.

PORT TACK: sailing course in which the booms are to starboard.

RUNNING: sailing before the wind.

SHEET IN: pull in with back hand to harden sail (opp.—sheet out).

STARBOARD: right side of boat when looking forward.

STARBOARD TACK: sailing course in which the booms are to port.

STERN: aft part of a boat.

TACK: (noun) the lower, forward corner of a sail.
(verb) (1) to work to windward by sailing on alternate courses, so the wind is first on one side of the boat, then on the other.
(2) to change tacks by turning head to wind (opp.—jibe).

WEATHER: windward.

WINDWARD: toward the direction from which the wind is coming (opp.—leeward).

YACHT: a general term for a vessel used exclusively for pleasure.

INDEX

PHOTO CREDITS

All black & white photographs by Roger Jones except for the following: photograph on page 12 courtesy of *Windsurfing International, Inc.*, Marina Del Rey, California, and photographs on page 118 courtesy of *The Honolulu Advertiser*. All color photographs by Steve Wilkings, Pacific Studios, Inc., Honolulu, Hawaii.

Freestyle Flow Chart on page 63 courtesy of *Windsurfing International, Inc.*, Marina Del Rey, California.

COLOR INSERT CAPTIONS

   i Larry Stanley at Kailua, Oahu

  ii Manuelle Graveline at Cancun, Mexico

 iii Pat Love & Dennis Davidson at Kailua, Oahu

 iv John Speer at Kailua, Oahu

  v Mark Robinson at Diamond Head, Oahu

 vi Ken Winner at Diamond Head, Oahu

 vii Cort Larned at Cancun, Mexico

viii Robby Naish at Kammieland, Oahu

 ix Larry Stanley at Diamond Head, Oahu

  x Hugh England Fly away at Diamond Head, Oahu

Front cover photograph:
Larry Stanley at Turtle Bay, Oahu

Back cover photograph:
Start of race at Cancun, Mexico